# Vegetarian Keto Diet
## Cookbook for Beginners

Quick & Easy Everyday Recipes
for Busy People on Keto Diet
#2019

Eva Foster

# CONTENTS

# INTRODUCTION

## The basics

It is no strange news that the ketogenic diet has come to stay having contributed a ton of benefits to the healthy eating lifestyle.

What better way to lose weight fast eating many delicious, creamy foods and still maintaining a good shape than with this offering.

In this book, I combine my favorite scrumptious keto treats and play on the no meat / no fish grounds. And the results turned out amazing!

Lots of them that get you eating with love year round. And just that you know, there's a lot of gooey-ness with these. Get your taste buds ready for them!

## The undenied pluses of the Ketogenic Diet

The ketogenic diet, which is a high-fat, moderate protein, and zero to low carb diet plays on the use of ingredients rich in healthy fats to suppress the body's intake of carbs. As a result, such benefits play out as such:

### *Blood Sugar Control*

Anything starchy is sugary. Frequent consumption of carbohydrates doesn't only bloat your body, but builds sugar levels. Meaning, diabetes may be strolling by if this isn't curbed.

The keto diet solves the problem with its carb reduction approach that leads to reduced sugar levels. By replacing carbs with fatty foods, the body suppresses the generation of sucrose in the body because fats contain almost no sugars.

### *Weight loss*

Of course! The body no longer burns carbs for energy, which would have stored up large quantities of fats in your body resulting in bloating.

On the keto diet, your body gets into a metabolic state known as ketosis where it is mandated to burn fat for energy because of the unavailability of carbohydrates.

Meanwhile, fats are a more effective way of burning energy than carbs; they burn efficiently and leave your body fuller for longer and feeling healthy always.

### *Appetite Control*

Carbs make you hungry often. Ever realized that? Not to say that you actually get hungry, but because carbs burn out fast, your body naturally pings you to fill up on more carbs frequently. The result is bad health in the end.

Fats don't do this – they are a slower burning energy form, keeping you satisfied for extended periods and curbing unnecessary appetites. And this saves you from weight gain problems.

### *Energy Levels*

Don't be deceived, carbs and sugars satisfy fast and burn faster. Hence, there are tendencies to feel extremely weak when on a high carb diet combined with heavy work schedules.

This happens because the body burns carbs quickly, which causes your energy levels to fluctuate making you less vibrant.

Meanwhile, high fats create a consistent level of energy as they burn gradually and in a steady manner.

### *Keto Diet and Insulin Resistance*

So, insulin is meant to be a good thing; I just thought I would clarify, but then there's a problem when the body becomes resistant to it.

On a high carb diet, the body processes starchy foods into glucose, which is transported to the muscles and tissues for energy through the vehicle called insulin.

However, when the body produces excess sugars, it becomes resistant to insulin, which then causes sugar to break free in the body. At this point, the liver and cells may stop absorbing the sugar in the body, which eventually finds its way into the blood and results in diabetes.

The keto diet prevents this from happening with its basic and natural carb reduction form.

## Should you eat little carbs on the ketogenic diet?

Yes, a very little carb is allowed, which should range from 20 to 50 grams per day.

There are a ton of low carb vegetables like cauliflower and broccoli that are healthy sources of carbohydrates on the ketogenic diet.

Reach for vegetables that grow above the ground because they a less sugar saturated. Below, I share some tasty options that you should choose from.

## Merging the ketogenic with the vegetarian diet.

A little secret –putting this cookbook has been one of my most loved so far. I love how the vegetarian diet is flexible allowing you to create recipes with delicious creams, nut milk, eggs, and everything fatty except meat and seafood.

For someone, which is crazy about cheese and not good with meat, the trick for making the healthiest combo meals was to play down on the carbs and embrace all the fatty ingredients that I need. So, to get your diet right, do these:

1.  Eat your cheeses, creams, nuts, seeds, oils, nut milk, etc. in generous quantities.

2.  Make sure to eat no more than 50 grams of carbohydrates in a day. My safest bet is 35 grams daily, especially for beginners.

3.  Grab all the low-carb vegetables that you can find. Splurge on greens and more greens.

4.  Drink a lot of water to keep you hydrated and full for longer.

5.  Also, take safe supplements and vitamins mostly to fill up the fruits that you will be missing.

## Now, to what you should be eating.

*   Vegan meats and seafood – for the many times when a recipe may require some meat, kindly swap them with tofu, tempeh, seitan, and other high-protein and low carb generated vegan meats. They taste good!

*   Leafy greens – never exclude collards, kale, spinach, and all types of fresh greens from your diet. They aren't only nutritious, but they are delicious.

- Dairy products – oh yes! Splurge on them with no guilt whatsoever. This is how you build your macros. Fill your fridge with cheeses, nut milk (not regular milk because it has many sugars in there), double cream, heavy cream, cream cheese, etc.

- Nuts and seeds – these should be your BFFs; walnuts, macadamia nuts, almonds, pistachios, peanuts, sunflower seeds, chia seeds, flax seeds, pumpkin seeds, etc.

- Above the ground vegetables – most vegetables that grow above the ground are mostly low in carbs. On the keto diet, zucchinis, broccoli, mushrooms, and cauliflower are the safest options.

- Fruits – meanwhile in this world, many fruits will have to be avoided because they are high in sugars. The safe keto options are olives, avocado, lemons, lime, and berries like strawberries, blueberries, blackberries, raspberries, etc.

- Oils and butter – use them as much as you desire; olive oil, coconut oil, avocado oil, sesame oil, MCT oil, butter, ghee, etc.

- Sea vegetables – like above the ground greens, these are also highly nutritious and contain close to zero carbs; kelp, dulse, bladderwrack, etc.

- Low carb sweeteners – swap the sugars and sweeteners for erythritol, stevia, monk fruit, swerve sugar etc.

- Herbs and spices – the flavor is necessary. Use as many herbs and spices as you desire because they are carb – free and give you the treat of aroma that you deserve.

## And now, don't eat these.

- Grains – they are carbohydrates loaded - rice, wheat, cereal, corn, barley, quinoa, polenta, etc.

- Tubers – also alike, these are very rich in carbohydrates and sugars. Avoid potatoes, squash, carrots, cabbages, sweet potatoes, yam, plantain, etc.

- Sugary fruits – too bad, but these have to go. Bananas, grapes, plums, watermelon, apples, papaya, oranges, etc.

- Legumes – carb certified! They include peas, lentils, beans, etc.

## Other essential nutrients and where to source them

- **Calcium** – to get your calcium rather than from meat, eat many leafy greens, tofu, and green above the ground vegetables.

- **Amino acids & iron** – find these in tofu, seitan, tempeh, nuts, and seeds

- **Vitamin D** – you'll get them in mushrooms, nut milk, tofu, morning sunlight, plant-derived supplements

## Finally, check in with your doctor

While both diets are very safe to get on, it is still essential to consult your doctor before trying them. Most notably for pregnant women, if you have an ailment, allergies, or have health questions.

Seek counsel from the doctor, and once you have a go ahead (for those not sure), I will be right here with these amazing recipes to rock your world with great tastes.

Ready to dig into your first plate? Come with me!

## Mini Ricotta Cakes

Wouldn't you serve these at your next wine and dine? Mini bites with a lot of flavors, cheese, and texture that will spin heads. Meanwhile, they get ready quickly, try them ASAP.

**PREPARATION TIME: 10 MINUTES • COOKING TIME: 31 MINUTES • SERVES: 4**

### Ingredients:

1 tbsp olive oil
1 tbsp + 1 tbsp butter
2 garlic cloves, minced
1 small white onion, finely chopped
1 cup cauli rice
¼ cup white wine
¼ cup vegetable stock
2 scallions, chopped

Salt and black pepper to taste
¼ cup grated parmesan cheese
½ cup ricotta cheese
1 tbsp sunflower oil
1 cup almond flour
½ cup golden flaxseed meal
2 eggs

### Directions:

Heat the olive oil and one tablespoon of butter in a medium saucepan over medium heat. Stir in the garlic and onion and cook until fragrant and soft, 3 minutes.

Mix in the cauli rice and allow flavoring for 30 seconds; add the wine, stir, allow reduction and absorption into the rice. Mix in the vegetable stock, scallions, salt, black pepper, remaining butter, parmesan cheese, and ricotta cheese. Cover the pot and cook until the liquid reduces and the rice thickens.

Open the lid, stir to incorporate the cheese fully, and spoon the mixture into a bowl to cool. Mold the dough into mini patties, about 14 to 16 and set aside.

Heat the sunflower oil in a medium skillet over medium heat; meanwhile pour the almond flour onto a plate, the golden flaxseed meal in another, and beat the eggs in a medium bowl.

Lightly dredge each patty in the flour, then in eggs, and then coated accurately in the flaxseed meal. Fry in the oil until compacted and golden brown, 2 minutes on each side. Transfer to a paper towel-lined plate, plate, and garnish with some scallions.

Serve warm with blue cheese dipping sauce.

### Nutritional Fact per Serving:

Calories: 362; Fat: 29.7g; Total Carbs: 13.2g; Fiber: 7g; Net Carbs: 6.2g; Protein: 13.3g

# Blackberry Camembert Puffs

So, I'd had camembert in a dip, baked in its case, but these puffs blew my mind. Are you looking for a way to surprise your guests? Hide these cubes of camembert in puff pastry and cover them up with blackberry sauce. Stay chilled to receive nice compliments.

**PREPARATION TIME: 10 MINUTES • COOKING TIME: 21 MINUTES • SERVES: 4**

## Ingredients:

*For the pastry cups:*

¼ cup almond flour + extra for dusting
3 tbsp coconut flour
½ tsp xanthan gum
½ tsp salt
4 tbsp cream cheese, room temperature
1/4 teaspoon cream of tartar

¼ cup butter, cold and crumbled
3 whole eggs, unbeaten
3 tbsp erythritol
1 ½ tsp vanilla extract
1 whole egg, beaten

*For the filling:*

1 tsp butter
1 yellow onion, finely chopped
3 tbsp red wine
1 tbsp balsamic vinegar

5 tbsp erythritol
½ cup fresh blackberries
5 oz Camembert, sliced and cut into 16 cubes
Freshly parsley leaves to garnish

## Directions:

*For the filling:*

Preheat the oven to 350 F, turn a muffin tray upside down and lightly grease with cooking spray.

In a large bowl, mix the almond flour, coconut flour, xanthan gum, and salt.

Add the cream cheese, cream of tartar, and butter; mix with an electric hand mixer until crumbly. Add the erythritol and vanilla extract until mixed. Then, pour in three of the eggs one after another while mixing until formed into a ball.

Flatten the dough on a clean flat surface, cover in plastic wrap, and refrigerate for 1 hour.

After, lightly dust a clean flat surface with almond flour, unwrap the dough, and roll out the dough into a large rectangle, ½ - inch thickness. Cut the dough into 16 squares and press each piece onto each muffin mound on the tray to form a bowl shape. Brush with the remaining eggs and bake in the oven until golden and puffed up, 10 minutes.

Remove from the oven, take the pastry cups off the tray and set aside to cool.

*For the filling:*

Melt the butter in a medium skillet over low heat and sauté the onion until softened, 3 minutes. Stir in the red wine, balsamic vinegar, erythritol, and blackberries. Cook until the berries become jammy and the wine reduces, 10 minutes. Turn the heat off and set aside.

Take out the tray and place a cheese cube in each pastry. Return to the oven and bake until the cheese melts, 2 to 3 minutes.

Remove the food and spoon a teaspoon each of the blackberry sauce on top.

Garnish with some parsley and serve immediately with chilled white wine.

## Nutritional Fact per Serving:

Calories: 372; Fat: 32.11g; Total Carbs: 5.9g; Fiber: 1.5g; Net Carbs: 4.4g; Protein: 14.4g

# Tofu Pops

I wouldn't tell you to wrap your tofu in bacon if it didn't taste dang good. Adding some tang, herby flavor, and the aroma from vegan bacon brings that scrumptious want-to-have-already.

**PREPARATION TIME: 1 HOUR 5 MINUTES • COOKING TIME: 12 MINUTES • SERVES: 4**

## Ingredients:

1 (14 oz) block extra firm tofu
1 small bunch chives, chopped
1 lemon, zested and juiced

12 slices vegan bacon, unsweetened
12 mini skewers
1 tsp butter

## Directions:

Place the tofu in between two paper towels and allow to drain liquid for 5 minutes.

Remove the napkins and cut the tofu into 12 blocks. Mix the chives, lemon zest, and juice in a bowl and toss the tofu cubes in the mixture. Allow marinating for 1 hour.

Remove the zest and chives off the cubes and wrap each tofu in a bacon slice; insert each skewer and the end of the bacon.

Melt the butter in a medium skillet over medium heat and fry the tofu skewers in the butter until the bacon browns and crisps. Transfer to a paper towel-lined plate to drain fat.

Transfer to a serving plate, remove the skewers (optional), garnish with chives, and serve with balsamic mayo dipping sauce.

## Nutritional Fact per Serving:

Calories: 392; Fat: 24.92g; Total Carbs: 11.4g; Fiber: 2.4g; Net Carbs: 9g; Protein: 18.12g

# Tofu Jalapeño Poppers

Classic labor of heat! Instead, minced tofu adds some filling texture to the poppers and loaded with all the essentials; cream cheese, herbs, scallions, and then served with a whopping creamy dip.

**PREPARATION TIME: 10 MINUTES • COOKING TIME: 20 MINUTES • SERVES: 4**

## Ingredients:

*For the poppers:*

1 tbsp olive oil
4 oz firm tofu, chopped in bits
1 garlic clove, minced
½ cup cream cheese
1 lemon, zested with 1 tsp juice
4 scallions, finely chopped
2 tbsp chopped cilantro
Salt and black pepper to taste
6 jalapeño peppers
3 tbsp grated cheddar cheese

*For the dip:*

1 tsp lemon juice
1 cup sour cream
1 tbsp chopped cilantro

## Directions:

Preheat the oven to 370 F.

Heat the olive oil in a small skillet over medium heat and fry the tofu until golden. Turn the heat off and transfer the tofu to a bowl. Mix in the garlic, cream cheese, lemon zest, juice, scallions, cilantro, salt, and black pepper.

Cut the chilies into halves using a knife; scoop the seeds and membrane. Lightly grease a baking sheet with cooking spray and arrange the peppers on top. Fill the jalapeño peppers with the cheese-tofu mixture and sprinkle with the cheddar cheese.

Bake in the oven for 15 minutes or until the cheese is golden brown.

While baking the peppers, in a small bowl, mix the lemon juice, sour cream, cilantro, and season with salt and black pepper.

Remove the peppers when ready and serve with the dip.

## Nutritional Fact per Serving:

Calories: 247; Fat: 21g; Total Carbs: 8.04g; Fiber: 1.1g; Net Carbs: 6.9g; Protein: 9.1g

# Sweet Tahini Twists

Don't bore yourself any further with basic twist pastry. If having them on the keto diet, fill with tahini and a generous sprinkle of sesame seeds. The flavor is checked and taste guaranteed. Preparation Time: 10 minutes

**COOKING TIME: 15 MINUTES • SERVES: 4**

## Ingredients:

*For the puff pastry:*

¼ cup almond flour + extra for dusting
3 tbsp coconut flour
½ tsp xanthan gum
½ tsp salt
4 tbsp cream cheese, room temperature
1/4 teaspoon cream of tartar

¼ cup butter, cold
3 whole eggs
3 tbsp erythritol
1 ½ tsp vanilla extract
1 whole egg, beaten

*For the filling:*

2 tbsp maple (sugar-free) syrup
3 tbsp tahini
2 tbsp sesame seeds

1 egg, beaten
2 tbsp poppy seeds
Sea salt for topping

## Directions:

Preheat the oven to 350 F and line a baking tray with parchment paper.

In a large bowl, mix the almond flour, coconut flour, xanthan gum, and salt.

Add the cream cheese, cream of tartar, and butter; mix with an electric hand mixer until crumbly. Add the erythritol and vanilla extract until mixed. Then, pour in 3 of the eggs one after another while mixing until formed into a ball.

Flatten the dough on a clean flat surface, cover in plastic wrap, and refrigerate for 1 hour.

After, lightly dust a clean flat surface with almond flour, unwrap the dough, and roll out the dough into a large rectangle, ½ - inch thickness.

In a small bowl, mix the maple (sugar-free) syrup with tahini and spread the mixture over the pastry. Sprinkle with half of the sesame seeds and cut the dough into 16 thin strips with ½ - inch thickness. Fold each strip in half.

Brush the top with the remaining egg, sprinkle with the remaining seeds, poppy seeds, and a little sea salt. Twist the pastry three to four times into straws and place on the baking sheet. Bake in the oven until golden brown, 15 minutes. Remove onto plates and serve with chocolate sauce.

## Nutritional Fact per Serving:

Calories: 348; Fat: 31.5g; Total Carbs: 5.7g; Fiber: 2.5g; Net Carbs: 3.16g; Protein: 11.7g

# Feta Cheese Choux Buns

Feta in these almond flour based buns is very keto approved. Once you taste this gooey treat, you'll definitely want to experiment with different types of cheese.

**PREPARATION TIME: 15 MINUTES • COOKING TIME: 25 MINUTES • SERVES: 4**

## Ingredients:

1 cup water
½ tsp salt
6 tbsp butter
2/3 cup almond flour
3 eggs, beaten
1 tbsp olive oil

2 white onions, thinly sliced
2 sprigs rosemary, leaves extracted
2 tbsp red wine vinegar
1 tsp swerve brown sugar
1 cup crumbled feta cheese
½ cup heavy whipping cream

## Directions:

Preheat the oven to 350 F and line a baking tray with parchment paper.

In a medium saucepan over medium temperature, heat the water, salt, and butter while occasionally stirring until the butter melts. Bring just to a boil and sift in the flour while beating vigorously with a wooden spoon until ball forms.

Turn the heat off; keep beating while adding the eggs, one at a time until the dough is smooth and slightly thickened.

Using a tablespoon, scoop mounds of the dough onto the baking dish. Dip your hands in cold water and press a hole in the center of each mound.

Bake in the oven for 20 minutes or until risen and golden. Remove from the oven and pierce the sides of the buns with a toothpick. Return to the oven and bake for 2 more minutes or until crispy. Remove after and place aside to cool.

Once cooled, tear out the middle part of the bun (keep the torn out part) to create a hole in the bun for the cream filling. Set aside

Heat the olive oil in a small saucepan and sauté the onions and rosemary for 2 minutes. Stir in the swerve brown sugar, red wine vinegar, and cook to bubble for 2 to 3 minutes or until caramelized. Turn the heat off and set aside to cool.

In a bowl, beat the whipping cream and feta cheese together and season with black pepper. Spoon the mixture into a piping bag and press a spoonful of the mixture into the buns. Cover with the torn out portion of pastry and top with the onion relish and serve immediately.

## Nutritional Fact per Serving:

Calories: 384; Fat: 37.32g; Total Carbs: 2.6g; Fiber: 0.1g; Net Carbs: 2.5g; Protein: 10.01g

# Avocado Pate with Flaxseed Toasts

My perfect alternative for sardine pate, which rocks in all its senses. Though ripe avocados give the ideal texture, mashing them with Greek yogurt creates a smoother, creamier, and richer consistency. They serve well with low carb crackers, toasts, and vegetable sticks.

**PREPARATION TIME: 5 MINUTES • SERVES: 4**

## Ingredients:

*For the flaxseed toasts:*

1/2 cup flaxseed meal
1/8 cup water

1 pinch salt

*For the Avocado pate:*

3 ripe avocados
4 tbsp Greek yogurt
2 tbsp chopped green onions

1 lemon, ½ tsp zest + 1 tsp juice
Black pepper to taste
Smoked paprika to garnish

## Directions:

*For the flaxseed toasts:*

Preheat your oven to 350 F.

Preheat a skillet to medium-high heat.

Mix the flaxseed meal, water, and salt in the preheated skillet using a spatula to mix continually and form the dough into a ball.

Place the dough in between two parchment papers, put on a flat surface, and flatten the dough thinly with a rolling pin. Remove the papers and cut the pastry into tortilla chips.

Place on a baking sheet and bake in the oven for 8-12 minutes or until crispy.

*For the avocado pate:*

Cut the avocados into halves, remove the pit, and scoop the pulp into a bowl.

Mix in the yogurt, green onions, lemon zest, juice, and black pepper until evenly combined.

Spread the pate on the toasts and garnish with the paprika.

Serve immediately.

## Nutritional Fact per Serving:

Calories: 364; Fat: 31.47g; Total Carbs: 19.9g; Fiber: 15.9g; Net Carbs: 4g; Protein: 7.42g

# Mediterranean Deviled Eggs

Add some life to your deviled eggs. How about with a Mediterranean touch?
Turmeric, feta, chili, and paprika are all your need. Try them as appetizers or as a
snack; they are delectable.

**PREPARATION TIME: 10 MINUTES • COOKING TIME: 17 MINUTES • SERVES: 6**

## Ingredients:

6 large eggs
1 cup water
Ice water bath
1 tsp Dijon mustard
3 tbsp mayonnaise
1 tsp white wine vinegar

2 tbsp crumbled feta cheese
¼ tsp turmeric powder
1 small red chili, deseeded and minced
1 tbsp chopped parsley + extra for garnishing
Salt and black pepper to taste
Smoked paprika to garnish

## Directions:

Boil the eggs in the water in a medium pot over high heat for 10 minutes. Drain the liquid and transfer the eggs to the ice water bath. Allow cooling for 5 minutes, peel and slice eggs in half.

Remove the yolks into a medium bowl and put the whites on a serving plate. Mash the yolks with a fork and mix in the mustard, mayonnaise, vinegar, feta cheese, turmeric, red chili, parsley, salt, and black pepper until evenly combined.

Spoon the mixture into a piping bag and fill into the egg whites.

Garnish with some parsley and paprika. Serve immediately.

## Nutritional Fact per Serving:

Calories: 139; Fat: 8.26g; Total Carbs: 1.21g; Fiber: 0.2g; Net Carbs: 1.01g; Protein: 7.6g

# Seeds Breakfast Loaf

Having bread on the keto diet is one of the hardest ever, but this all seed loaf makes things a lot yummier. My favorite part; the crunchy bite into varying seeds that you get.

**PREPARATION TIME: 8 MINUTES • COOKING TIME: 45 MINUTES • SERVES: 6**

## Ingredients:

¾ cup coconut flour
1 cup almond flour
3 tbsp baking powder
2 tbsp psyllium husk powder
2 tbsp desiccated coconut
5 tbsp sesame seeds
¼ cup flaxseed
¼ cup hemp seeds

1 tsp ground caraway seeds
1 tbsp poppy seeds
1 tsp salt
1 tsp mixed spice
6 eggs
2/3 cup cream cheese, at room temperature
¾ cup heavy cream
4 tbsp sesame oil

## Directions:

Preheat the oven to 350 F.

In a large bowl, mix the coconut flour, almond flour, baking powder, psyllium husk powder, desiccated coconut, sesame seeds, flaxseed, hemp seeds, ground caraway, poppy seeds, salt, and mixed spice.

In a smaller bowl, whisk the eggs, cream cheese, heavy cream, and sesame oil. Pour the mixture into the dry ingredients and combine both into a smooth dough.

Grease a loaf pan with cooking spray and pour in the dough. Bake in the oven for 45 minutes or until a toothpick inserted into the bread comes out clean.

Take out the pan, remove the bread onto a rack, and allow cooling.

Slice the bread and serve for breakfast.

## Nutritional Fact per Serving:

Calories: 584; Fat: 50g; Total Carbs: 14.6g; Fiber: 7g; Net Carbs: 7.49g; Protein: 23.3g

# Croque Madame with Pesto

This pleasant French delicacy never got tastier without pesto. That's why I add some to the classic to improve the flavor while using vegan ham. Up for some? You'll be thankful you made it.

**PREPARATION TIME: 15 MINUTES • COOKING TIME: 30 MINUTES • SERVES: 4**

## Ingredients:

### For the béchamel:

2 tbsp unsalted butter
1 cup almond milk + extra as needed
2 tbsp almond flour

Salt and black pepper to season
½ tsp nutmeg powder
4 tbsp grated Monterey Jack cheese

### For the pesto:

½ cup basil leaves
1/3 cup toasted pine nuts
¼ cup grated parmesan cheese

1 garlic clove, peeled
¼ cup olive oil

### For the sandwich:

2 tbsp melted butter
4 slices low carb bread
1 (7 oz) can sliced mushrooms, drained
3 medium tomatoes, sliced

4 slices mozzarella cheese
1 tbsp olive oil
4 large whole eggs
Baby arugula for garnishing

## Directions:

### For the béchamel sauce:

Heat the butter and half of the milk in a medium saucepan over medium heat. When the butter melts, whisk in the remaining milk with flour until smooth roux forms.

Season with salt, black pepper, and nutmeg. Reduce the heat to low and stir in the Monterey Jack cheese until melted. Turn the heat off and set the sauce aside.

### For the pesto:

In a food processor, puree the basil, pine nuts, Parmesan, garlic, and olive oil.

Transfer to a glass jar, cover the lid, and refrigerate until ready to use.

### For the sandwich:

Preheat the grill to medium-high.

Brush both sides of each bread with butter and toast each on both sides until golden.

Remove onto a plate and spread the béchamel sauce on one side of each bread, then the pesto, and divide the mushrooms, tomatoes, and mozzarella cheese on top of each bread.

One after the other, return each sandwich to the grill and cook until the cheese melts. Transfer to serving plates.

Heat the olive oil in a skillet over medium heat and crack an egg into the oil. Cook until the whites are set but the yolks still soft and runny. Place the egg on a sandwich and repeat the same process for the remaining eggs for the rest of the sandwich.

Season with salt and black pepper, and garnish with the arugula. Serve warm.

## Nutritional Fact per Serving:

Calories: 630; Fat: 55g; Total Carbs: 10.5g; Fiber: 6.8g; Net Carbs: 3.7g; Protein: 25.3g

# Blackberry Chia Pudding

What better way to make a pudding tastier than with coconut milk and fresh blackberries. It is creamy, thick, and rich with a garnish of almonds.

**PREPARATION TIME: 15 MINUTES • COOKING TIME: 30 MINUTES • SERVES: 4**

## Ingredients:

1 ½ cups coconut milk
½ cup Greek yogurt
4 tsp maple (sugar-free) syrup
1 tsp vanilla extract
7 tbsp chia seeds

1 cup fresh blackberries (reserving a few to garnish)
Chopped almonds to garnish
Mint leaves to garnish

## Directions:

In a bowl, combine the coconut milk, Greek yogurt, maple (sugar-free) syrup, and vanilla extract until evenly combined. Mix in the chia seeds.

Puree the blackberries in a bowl using a fork and stir the puree into the yogurt mixture.

Share the mixture into four medium mason jars, cover the lids and refrigerate for 30 minutes to thicken the pudding.

Remove the jars, take off the lid, and stir the mixture. Garnish with two blackberries each, almonds, and some mint leaves.

Serve immediately.

## Nutritional Fact per Serving:

Calories: 309; Fat: 26g; Total Carbs: 15.67g; Fiber: 8.8g; Net Carbs: 6.87g; Protein: 7.1g

# Blueberry Soufflé

Realizing that omelet merges well with fruits was one of the best things that I ever found. You can imagine how creative I get. This blueberry omelet is an asset of tastes to behold.

**PREPARATION TIME: 15 MINUTES • COOKING TIME: 20 MINUTES • SERVES: 4**

## Ingredients:

*For the blueberry sauce:*

1 cup frozen blueberries
2 tsp erythritol

1 tbsp water

*For the omelet:*

4 egg yolks, room temperature
3 tbsp erythritol, divided
3 egg whites, room temperature

1 tsp olive oil
½ lemon, zested to garnish

## Directions:

*For the blueberry sauce:*

Pour the blueberries, erythritol and water in a small saucepan over medium heat. Cook with occasional stirring until the berries soften and become syrupy, 8 to 10 minutes. Stir in the vanilla, turn the heat off, and set aside to cool slightly.

*For the omelet:*

Preheat the oven to 350 F.

In a large bowl, beat the egg yolks and 1 tablespoon of erythritol with an electric whisk until thick and pale. In another bowl, whisk the egg whites at low speed with clean beaters until foamy. Increase the speed, add the remaining erythritol, 1 tablespoon at a time, and whisk until soft peak forms, 3 to 4 minutes. Gently and gradually, fold the egg white mixture into the egg yolk mix.

Heat the olive oil in a safe oven non-stick frying pan over low heat. Swirl the pan to spread the oil and pour in the egg mixture; swirl to spread too. Cook for 3 minutes and then, transfer to the oven; bake for 2 to 3 minutes or until golden, puffed, and set.

Plate the omelet and spoon the blueberry sauce onto the egg. Use the spoon to spread around. Garnish with lemon zest. Serve immediately with tea or coffee.

## Nutritional Fact per Serving:

Calories: 99; Fat: 5.94g; Total Carbs: 3.92g; Fiber: 1.1g; Net Carbs: 2.82g; Protein: 5.58g

# Coconut Waffles with Cranberries

The best part of making waffles with coconut flour is the flavor and texture that you get. They turn out crunchy, puffed, soft, and sweet. Greek yogurt with cranberry puree add on some fatty essentials with some needed tang.

**PREPARATION TIME: 6 MINUTES • COOKING TIME: 10 MINUTES • SERVES: 4**

## Ingredients:

2/3 cup coconut flour
2 ½ tsp baking powder
A pinch salt
2 eggs
1 ½ cups almond milk
6 tbsp unsalted butter + extra for greasing (melted and cooled slightly)
Natural yogurt for topping

*Cranberry puree for topping:*

¼ cup fresh cranberries
2/3 cup erythritol
3/4 cup water
1 tsp lemon zest
1/2 tsp vanilla extract

## Directions:

In a bowl, mix the coconut flour, baking powder, and salt. In another bowl, whisk the eggs, milk, and butter and pour the mixture into the flour mix. Combine until a smooth batter forms.

Preheat a waffle iron and brush with butter. When ready, pour some of the batter (in batches) onto hot waffles iron, close, and cook until golden and crisp, 2 to 3 minutes.

Plate the waffles, spoon a dollop of yogurt on top and followed by the cranberry puree.

*To make the cranberry topping:*

Add the cranberries, erythritol, water, and lemon zest in a medium saucepan. Bring to a boil over medium heat and then reduce the temperature to simmer for 10 to 15 minutes or until the cranberries break and a sauce forms.

## Nutritional Fact per Serving:

Calories: 247; Fat: 21g; Total Carbs: 12.9g; Fiber: 5.9g; Net Carbs: 6.9g; Protein: 6.63g

# Almond-Berry Pancakes with Sweet Syrup

When these fluffy, pink pancakes are set and ready, you'll be awed that you made them yourself. They taste good with the various toppings: yogurt, berries, and sweet syrup.

**PREPARATION TIME: 10 MINUTES • COOKING TIME: 15 MINUTES • SERVES: 4**

## Ingredients:

½ cup almond flour
1 tsp baking soda
A pinch salt
1 tbsp swerve sugar
A pinch cinnamon powder

1 handful of strawberries and raspberries, mashed
1 egg
½ cup almond milk
2 tsp butter

*For the topping:*

1 handful fresh strawberries and raspberries
1 cup Greek yogurt

Stevia for serving

## Directions:

In a medium bowl, combine the almond flour, baking soda, salt, swerve sugar, and cinnamon powder. Whisk in the mashed berries, and egg, and mix in the milk until smooth.

Melt ½ teaspoon of butter in a non-stick skillet over medium heat and pour in a tablespoon of the mixture into the pan. Swirl the pan quickly to spread the batter. Cook until small bubbles appear on top, flip, and cook until golden.

Transfer to a plate and proceed with using up the remaining batter for pancakes.

Place pancakes in serving plates and top with yogurt, berries, and stevia. Serve immediately.

## Nutritional Fact per Serving:

Calories: 194; Fat: 14.8g; Total Carbs: 9.6g; Fiber: 2g; Net Carbs: 7.6g; Protein: 7.6g

# Toast Sticks with Yogurt Berry Bowls

A more satisfying breakfast option when you have a heavily tasked day ahead. This will last you until lunchtime and provides you with your morning macros as needed.

**PREPARATION TIME: 6 MINUTES • COOKING TIME: 8 MINUTES • SERVES: 2**

## Ingredients:

*For the salad:*

2 cups Greek yogurt
2 tbsp maple (sugar-free) syrup
½ cup strawberries, halved

½ cup blueberries
½ cup raspberries

*For the toasts sticks:*

2 eggs
A pinch cinnamon powder
A pinch nutmeg powder
2 tbsp almond milk

Salt and black pepper to taste
4 slices low carb bread
1 ½ tbsp butter
1 tbsp olive oil

## Directions:

*For the salad:*

In a medium bowl, mix the yogurt, maple syrup, and berries. Chill the salad for about an hour.

*For the toasts:*

In a bowl, whisk the eggs, cinnamon, nutmeg, milk, salt, and black pepper. Set aside.

Cut each slice into four strips. Set aside. Heat the butter and olive oil in a non-stick skillet. Dip each bread strip into the egg mixture and fry in the olive oil, flipping once until golden brown on both sides. Once ready, transfer to a serving plate and serve with the yogurt berry salad.

## Nutritional Fact per Serving:

Calories: 207; Fat: 14.3g; Total Carbs: 13g; Fiber: 9.8g; Net Carbs: 3.3g; Protein: 7.7g

# Strawberry, Walnut & Pecan Porridge

Why I like porridges? You can top with everything that you like. For a keto make, strawberries, walnuts & pecans blend perfectly. Enjoy with a lot of heartiness.

**PREPARATION TIME: 8 MINUTES • COOKING TIME: 15 MINUTES • SERVES: 2**

## Ingredients:

2 tbsp coconut flour
1 tsp psyllium husk powder
Salt to taste
6 tbsp heavy whipping cream
2 oz butter
2 eggs

2 tbsp freshly squeezed lemon juice
1 tsp cinnamon powder
6 fresh strawberries, halved
4 tbsp chopped walnuts
2 tbsp chopped pecans

## Directions:

In a medium saucepan, combine the coconut flour, psyllium husk powder, salt, whipping cream, butter, egg, lemon juice, and cinnamon powder. Cook the ingredients over low heat while stirring constantly but do not allow boiling until thickened.

Dish the porridge and top with the strawberries, walnuts, and pecans. Serve warm.

## Nutritional Fact per Serving:

Calories: 588; Fat: 58g; Total Carbs: 9.4g; Fiber: 3.3g; Net Carbs: 6.1g; Protein: 11.5g

# Avocado Halloumi Scones

I will have these scones any day because they are creamy and delicious. Quite simple to make, they turn out crunchy on the outside, but soft and salivating when broken into.

**PREPARATION TIME: 8 MINUTES • COOKING TIME: 25 MINUTES • SERVES: 4**

## Ingredients:

2 cups almond flour
3 tsp baking powder
½ cup butter, cold
1 cup crumbled halloumi cheese

1 ripe avocado, pitted and mashed
1 large egg
1/3 cup buttermilk

## Directions:

Preheat the oven to 350 F and line a baking sheet with parchment paper.

In a large bowl, combine the almond flour and baking powder. Add the butter and mix with your hands. Top with the halloumi, avocado, and combine again.

Lightly whisk the egg with the buttermilk and slowly stir in the mixture into the halloumi mix using a fork. Mold 8 to 10 scones out to the batter.

Place the scones on the baking sheet and bake in the oven for 20 to 25 minutes or until the scones turn a golden color.

Remove; allow cooling for 5 minutes, and serve.

## Nutritional Fact per Serving:

Calories: 432; Fat: 41.9g; Total Carbs: 5.8g; Fiber: 3.4g; Net Carbs: 2.3g; Protein: 10.8g

# Breakfast Ratatouille with Eggs & Avocado

No ratatouille layering required: sauté all the vegetables in oil, cook in tomato sauce, and then further with some eggs. Voilà! Goodness at your disposal.

**PREPARATION TIME: 15 MINUTES • COOKING TIME: 32 MINUTES • SERVES: 2**

## Ingredients:

1 tbsp olive oil
1 zucchini, trimmed and sliced
1 medium red onion, trimmed and sliced
1 red bell pepper, deseeded and sliced
1 yellow bell pepper, deseeded and sliced
2 medium tomatoes, diced

1 cup vegetable broth
Salt and black pepper to taste
4 eggs
1 ripe avocado, pitted and chopped
2 tbsp chopped parsley to garnish

## Directions:

Heat the olive oil in a medium skillet over medium heat and sauté the zucchini, onion, and bell peppers until golden and beginning to soften, 10 minutes.

Pour in the tomatoes, vegetable broth, and season with salt and black pepper. Bring to a boil and then simmer until the sauce thickens slightly and the vegetables soft.

Use a wooden spoon to create four holes in the sauce and break an egg into each hole. Allow the eggs to cook through and turn the heat off. Plate the sauce, top with the avocado, and garnish with parsley. Serve immediately with creamy sesame bread slices.

## Nutritional Fact per Serving:

Calories: 450; Fat: 31.8g; Total Carbs: 17.8g; Fiber: 12g; Net Carbs: 5.6g; Protein: 18.4g

# Shakshuka

Is this shakshuka worth having for breakfast? Yes, it certainly is. However, you will need to reduce the amount of chili for it. And be explorative with your toppings; herbs, yogurt, and some cheese (as desired) to make it more exciting.

**PREPARATION TIME: 10 MINUTES • COOKING TIME: 27 MINUTES • SERVES: 2**

## Ingredients:

1 tsp olive oil
1 garlic clove, minced
1 small white onion, chopped
1 medium red bell pepper, deseeded and chopped
1 small green chili, deseeded and minced
1 cup diced tomatoes
½ cup unsweetened tomato sauce
Salt and black pepper to taste

1 tsp cumin powder
1/3 cup baby kale, chopped
½ tsp dried basil
4 large eggs
Freshly chopped parsley to garnish
¼ cup yogurt
½ lemon, juiced

## Directions:

Heat the olive oil in a medium deep skillet and sauté the garlic, onion, bell pepper, and green chili until softened, 5 minutes. Stir in the tomatoes, tomato sauce, salt, black pepper, and cumin; cover and cook for 10 minutes.

Add the kale to wilt and stir in the basil. Create four holes in the sauce with a wooden spoon, crack an egg into each hole, and sprinkle with parsley. Cover with a lid and cook until the eggs are firm, 8 to 10 minutes.

Meanwhile, in a bowl, mix the yogurt with lemon juice and set aside. Plate the shakshuka, top with a generous dollop of yogurt mixture, and serve with sliced avocados.

## Nutritional Fact per Serving:

Calories: 320; Fat: 16.9g; Total Carbs: 17g; Fiber: 9.3g; Net Carbs: 8g; Protein: 16.9g

# Vanilla Buttermilk Pancakes

The buttermilk helps puff up the pancakes; the almond flour, vanilla caviar, and lemon juice infuse the batter with lots of flavors. This is a given!

**PREPARATION TIME: 8 MINUTES • COOKING TIME: 15 MINUTES • SERVES: 4**

## Ingredients:

½ cup almond flour
½ tsp baking powder
1 tbsp swerve sugar
½ cup buttermilk
1 lemon, juiced
3 eggs

1 vanilla pod
2 tbsp unsalted butter
2 tbsp olive oil
Maple syrup (sugar-free) to serve
Greek yogurt to serve
Blueberries to serve

## Directions:

Into a bowl, sift the almond flour and baking powder and stir in the swerve sugar. In a small bowl, whisk the buttermilk, lemon juice, and eggs. Combine the mixture with the flour mix until smooth.

Cut the vanilla pod open and scrape the beans into the flour mixture. Stir to incorporate evenly.

In a skillet set over medium heat, melt a quarter each of the butter and olive oil and spoon in 1 ½ tablespoons of the pancake mixture into the pan. Cook for 3 to 4 minutes or until small bubbles begin to show. Flip the pancake and cook the other side for 2 minutes or until set and golden. Repeat cooking until the batter finishes using the remaining butter and olive oil in the same proportions.

Plate the pancakes, drizzle with maple syrup, top with a generous dollop of yogurt, and scatter some blueberries on top. Serve immediately.

## Nutritional Fact per Serving:

Calories: 168; Fat: 11g; Total Carbs: 10.3g; Fiber: 9g; Net Carbs: 1.6g; Protein: 7g

# Soy Chorizo, Goat Cheese, and Eggs

Whoever thought that sunshine eggs could be this engineered? Here you have it, a more exciting way to get your eggs beaming with richness.

**PREPARATION TIME: 10 MINUTES • COOKING TIME: 5 MINUTES • SERVES: 4**

## Ingredients:

1 tsp olive oil
1 tsp smoked paprika
3 oz soy chorizo, diced
4 eggs

½ cup crumbled goat cheese
2 green onions, thinly sliced diagonally
2 tbsp fresh parsley, chopped
Natural yogurt to serve

## Directions:

Preheat the oven to 350 F.

On a stovetop over medium temperature, heat the olive oil along with the paprika in an oven safe non-stick frying pan for 30 seconds. Add the soy chorizo and cook until lightly browned; spoon the soy chorizo into a bowl, leaving the olive oil in the pan.

Crack the eggs into the pan, cook for 2 minutes, and then sprinkle with the chorizo and crumble the goat cheese all around the egg white, but not on the yolks.

Transfer the pan to oven and bake for 2 more minutes, until the yolks are quite set, but still runny within. Remove the pan, garnish with the green onions and parsley. Serve warm with yogurt.

## Nutritional Fact per Serving:

Calories: 257; Fat: 18g; Total Carbs: 6.1g; Fiber: 0.5g; Net Carbs: 5.6g; Protein: 17.5g

# Gruyere Breakfast Soufflés

Whenever there is an opportunity to splurge on cheese, I am there with 100% attention. These soufflés are beauties to the eyes and to the tongue.

**PREPARATION TIME: 10 MINUTES • COOKING TIME: 10 MINUTES • SERVES: 4**

## Ingredients:

2 ½ tbsp butter, softened
2 ½ tbsp almond flour
1 ½ tsp mustard powder
½ cup almond milk

2 ½ cup Gruyere cheese, grated + a little extra for topping
4 yolks, beaten
2 egg whites, beaten until stiff

## Directions:

Preheat the oven to 375 F and brush the inner parts of four ramekins with some butter.

Melt the remaining 2 tablespoons of butter in a small pan over low heat and stir in the almond flour, cook for 1 minute, stirring constantly. Remove from the heat, mix in the mustard powder until evenly combined and slowly whisk in the milk until no lumps form.

Return to medium heat, while still stirring until the sauce comes to a rolling boil. Stir in the Gruyere cheese until melted. Turn the heat off.

Into the egg yolks whisk ¼ cup of the warmed milk mixture, then combine with the remaining milk sauce. Fold in the egg whites gradually until evenly combined.

Spoon the mixture into the ramekins and top with the remaining cheese. Bake for 8 minutes, until the soufflés have a slight wobble, but soft at the center. Allow cooling and serve.

## Nutritional Fact per Serving:

Calories: 488; Fat: 39g; Total Carbs: 4.1g; Fiber: 0.3g; Net Carbs: 3.8g; Protein: 29.6g

# Zucchini Muffins

Zucchinis are those ingredients that create a nice impression, however used. One or two of these muffins will keep you full until lunchtime or past it. Serve them with a creamy strawberry smoothie.

**PREPARATION TIME: 10 MINUTES • SERVES: 6**

## Ingredients:

½ cup almond flour
1 tsp baking powder
½ tsp baking soda
1 ½ tsp mustard powder
Salt and black pepper to taste
1/3 cup almond milk
1 large egg
5 tbsp olive oil
½ cup grated cheddar cheese
2 zucchinis, grated
6 green olives, pitted and sliced
1 spring onion, finely chopped
1 small red bell pepper, deseeded and chopped
1 tbsp freshly chopped thyme

## Directions:

Preheat the oven to 325 F and grease a pan with cooking spray.

In a large bowl, combine the almond flour, baking powder, baking soda, mustard powder, salt, black pepper. In a smaller bowl, whisk the milk, egg, and olive oil. Mix the wet ingredients into the dry ingredients and add the cheese, zucchini, olives, spring onion, bell pepper, and thyme. Combine well.

Spoon the batter into the muffin holes, ¾-inch full and bake in the oven for 30 to 35 minutes or until golden brown on top and skewer inserted comes out clean.

Remove the pan from the oven and allow the muffins to cool in a tin for 10 minutes before removing. Serve immediately for brunch.

## Nutritional Fact per Serving:

Calories: 172; Fat: 16.7g; Total Carbs: 2.2g; Fiber: 0.6g; Net Carbs: 1.6g; Protein: 3.9g

# SNACKS

## Basil-Chili Mozzarella Bites

A little touch of chili and herb creates a whole new delight for these bites. The result is an advancement in flavor and taste while offering all the right keto essentials.

**PREPARATION TIME: 5 MINUTES • COOKING TIME: 5 MINUTES • SERVES: 4**

### Ingredients:

1 cup olive oil, for frying
1 cup almond flour
½ tsp chili powder
1 tsp onion powder
1 tsp garlic powder
1 tsp dried basil
1 large egg
1 cup golden flaxseed meal
1 cup mozzarella cheese cubes
¼ cup small tomatoes, halved
A handful of fresh basil leaves

### Directions:

Heat the olive oil in a deep frying pan while you prepare the cheese for frying.

In a medium bowl, combine the almond flour, chili powder, onion powder, garlic powder, and basil. Set aside.

Lightly beat the egg in a small bowl and pour the flaxseed meal in a plate.

Coat each cheese cube in the flour mixture, then in the eggs, and then lightly in the golden flaxseed meal.

Fry in the hot oil until golden brown on both sides. Transfer to a wire rack to drain grease.

On each tomato half, place 1 basil leaf, top with a cheese cube each, and insert a toothpick through the middle of the sandwich to hold together.

Serve with marinara dipping sauce.

### Nutritional Fact per Serving:

Calories: 769; Fat: 73g; Total Carbs: 15g; Fiber: 12.5g; Net Carbs: 2.4g; Protein: 18.6g

# Cauliflower Chips with Cheese Dip

Just so, you aren't tempted to dip some regular biscuits into this cheese dip, I provide you with rich cauliflower chips for your indulgence. Both combined perfect an excellent ketogenic diet.

**PREPARATION TIME: 15 MINUTES • COOKING TIME: 20 MINUTES • SERVES: 6**

## Ingredients:

*For the cauliflower chips:*

1 medium head cauliflower, cut into florets
1 ½ cup water, for steaming
½ tsp salt or to taste

1 ½ tbsp almond flour
1 tbsp flax seeds
1 tbsp chia seeds

*For the cranberry cheese dip:*

8 oz cream cheese, softened
2 tbsp maple (sugar-free) syrup
¾ cup dried cranberries, chopped finely
¼ cup toasted almonds, finely chopped

¼ cup toasted pecans, finely chopped
3 tbsp chia seeds
1 tbsp lemon zest

## Directions:

*For the cauliflower chips:*

Preheat the oven to 350 F.

Pour the cauliflower and water in a medium pot and bring to a boil over medium heat until the vegetables are soft. Drain through a colander and transfer to a food processor; puree until very smooth.

Pour the mixture into a medium bowl and stir in the salt and almond flour until evenly combined. Mix in the flax seeds and chia seeds too.

Line a large baking sheet with parchment paper and spread in the batter. Cover with a plastic wrap and use a rolling pin to flatten and level the mixture evenly and lightly.

Take of the plastic wrap after and use a knife to cut our chip-size squares on the batter. Bake in the oven for 15 to 20 minutes or until the chips are golden brown and crispy. Remove, allow cooling for 5 minutes and transfer to a serving bowl.

*For the cheese dip:*

In a medium bowl, mix the cream cheese with the maple syrup until properly mixed. Add the cranberries, almonds, pecans, chia seeds, and lemon juice; combine evenly. Serve the dip immediately with the cauliflower chips.

## Nutritional Fact per Serving:

Calories: 252; Fat: 22.3g; Total Carbs: 9.2g; Fiber: 3g; Net Carbs: 6.2g; Protein: 6.5g

# Pesto Mushroom Pinwheels

Try these pinwheels with a spinach and mushroom filling. The outcome is worth the combination with pesto. Mind you, they satisfy for longer, so you want to have a few if you are hoping to have lunch soon.

**PREPARATION TIME: 15 MINUTES • COOKING TIME: 25 MINUTES + 10 MINUTES CHILLING • SERVES: 4**

## Ingredients:

*For the puff pastry:*

¼ cup almond flour + extra for dusting
3 tbsp coconut flour
½ tsp xanthan gum
½ tsp salt
4 tbsp cream cheese, room temperature
1/4 teaspoon cream of tartar

¼ cup butter, cold
3 whole eggs
3 tbsp erythritol
1 ½ tsp vanilla extract
1 whole egg, beaten

*For the filling:*

1 cup basil pesto (olive oil base)
2 cups baby spinach, steamed
2/3 cup canned mixed mushrooms, chopped

Salt and black pepper to taste
1 cup grated cheddar cheese
1 egg, beaten for brushing

## Directions:

In a large bowl, mix the almond flour, coconut flour, xanthan gum, and salt.

Add the cream cheese, cream of tartar, and butter; mix with an electric hand mixer until crumbly. Add the erythritol and vanilla extract until mixed in. Then, pour in 3 of the eggs one after another while mixing until formed into a ball.

Flatten the dough a clean flat surface, cover in plastic wrap, and refrigerate for 1 hour.

After, lightly dust a clean flat surface with almond flour, unwrap the dough, and roll out into 15 X 12 inches. Spread the pesto on top with a spatula leaving a 2-inch border on one end.

In a bowl, combine the spinach and mushrooms, season with salt and black pepper, and spread the mixture on the pesto. Sprinkle with the cheddar cheese and roll up as tightly as possible from a shorter end. Chill in the refrigerator for 10 minutes.

Meanwhile, preheat the oven to 380 F.

Remove the pastry onto a flat surface and use a sharp knife to into 24 slim discs. Arrange on the baking sheet, brush with the remaining egg, and bake in the oven for 20 to 25 minutes or until golden. Transfer onto a plate, allow cooling for 5 minutes, and serve with tomato dipping sauce.

## Nutritional Fact per Serving:

Calories: 535; Fat: 40.8g; Total Carbs: 4.8g; Fiber: 0.7g; Net Carbs: 4g; Protein: 34.6g

# Cheddar and Halloumi Sticks

Word of caution: make plenty because you'll keep eating them. It is one thing to fry cheese sticks in oil, but then it is a better idea to coat them in more cheese and bake them crispy good.

**PREPARATION TIME: 5 MINUTES • COOKING TIME: 10 MINUTES • SERVES: 6**

## Ingredients:

1/3 cup almond flour
2 tsp smoked paprika
1 lb halloumi, cut into 2-inch strips
½ cup grated cheddar cheese
2 tbsp chopped parsley
½ tsp cayenne powder

## Directions:

Preheat the oven to 350 F and grease a baking sheet with cooking spray.

In a small bowl, mix the flour with paprika and lightly dredge the halloumi in the mixture. Arrange on the baking sheet.

In a smaller bowl, combine the parsley, cheddar cheese, and cayenne powder. Sprinkle the mixture on the cheese and lightly grease with cooking spray.

Bake the cheese in the oven for 10 minutes or until golden brown.

Remove allow cooling for 3 minutes and serve with marinara dipping sauce.

## Nutritional Fact per Serving:

Calories: 886; Fat: 77.56g; Total Carbs: 20g; Fiber: 14g; Net Carbs: 6.1g; Protein: 13.8g

# All Seeds Flapjacks

Alternating non-keto fruits and oats with many seeds is an excellent way to enjoy flapjacks on the keto diet. These are crunchy and yummy.

**PREPARATION TIME: 5 MINUTES • COOKING TIME: 25 MINUTES • SERVES: 4**

## Ingredients:

6 tbsp salted butter
8 tbsp maple (sugar-free) syrup
8 tbsp swerve brown sugar
3 tbsp sesame seeds
3 tbsp chia seeds

3 tbsp hemp seeds
3 tbsp sunflower seeds
3 tbsp flax seeds
1 tbsp poppy seeds
4 tbsp dried goji berries, chopped

## Directions:

Preheat the oven to 350 F and line a baking sheet with parchment paper.

Melt the butter, maple syrup, and brown sugar in a small saucepan over low heat, stir gently and occasionally until the sugar dissolves.

Take the pan off the heat and stir in the sesame seeds, chia seeds, hemp seeds, sunflower seeds, flax seeds, poppy seeds, and goji berries until evenly combined.

Spread the mix into the baking sheet and bake in the oven for 20 minutes or until golden brown.

Remove after and slice the flapjacks into the 16 strips. Allow slight cooling and turn the flapjacks onto a chopping board. Divide into squares and cool completely. Serve.

## Nutritional Fact per Serving:

Calories: 300; Fat: 28g; Total Carbs: 8.5g; Fiber: 5.5g; Net Carbs: 3g; Protein: 6.8g

# Avocado Fries

When avocados are in season, it is an excellent idea to be explorative with them. These are simple, but turn out like a luxury. And of course, luxury is tasty.

**PREPARATION TIME: 5 MINUTES • COOKING TIME: 2 MINUTES • SERVES: 2**

## Ingredients:

½ cup olive oil
3 large avocados, halved and pitted
1 ½ tbsp almond flour

Salt and black pepper to taste
1 cup grated Parmesan cheese
2 large eggs

## Directions:

Heat the olive oil in a deep frying pan over medium heat.

Meanwhile, slice the avocados into 6 pieces each and set aside.

In a bowl, combine the almond flour, salt, black pepper, and parmesan. Set aside.

Crack the eggs into a medium bowl and beat lightly.

Toss the avocado slices in the egg and then generously dredge in the parmesan mixture.

Fry in the hot oil until golden brown, 1 to 2 minutes, and transfer to a wire rack.

Allow cooling for 1 minute and serve immediately with blue cheese dipping sauce.

## Nutritional Fact per Serving:

Calories: 849; Fat: 77.3g; Total Carbs: 21.2g; Fiber: 14g; Net Carbs: 7.2g; Protein: 21g

# Hemp Seeds Zucchini Chips

Here's a good place to give your zucchini chips a facelift. With some seeds, paprika, and chili, these crunches will be deserving of your afternoon.

**PREPARATION TIME: 5 MINUTES • COOKING TIME: 10 MINUTES • SERVES: 4**

## Ingredients:

4 large zucchinis, thinly sliced
4 tbsp olive oil
1 tsp smoked paprika

2 tbsp hemp seeds
2 tbsp poppy seeds
1 tsp red chili flakes

## Directions:

Preheat the oven to 350 F and place the zucchini in a colander. Sprinkle with salt and allow liquid draining for 5 minutes. Pat the zucchinis dry with a paper towel and transfer to a baking sheet.

Drizzle with olive oil, sprinkle with the paprika, and massage to spread the spice. Scatter with the hemp seeds, poppy seeds, and chili flakes. Season with salt, black pepper, and roast in the oven for 20 minutes or until crispy and golden brown.

Transfer to the serving basket and serve chips with marinara dipping sauce.

## Nutritional Fact per Serving:

Calories: 173; Fat: 17.7g; Total Carbs: 3g; Fiber: 1.6g; Net Carbs: 1.3g; Protein: 2.2g

# Herby Cheesy Nuts

And while I am about improving your snack options, to make your nuts more keto certified and exciting, pair them with some seeds, sweet, cheese, and herbs. You'll enjoy plenty of it.

**PREPARATION TIME: 5 MINUTES • COOKING TIME: 15 MINUTES • SERVES: 4**

## Ingredients:

1 egg white
4 tsp yeast extract
1 tsp swerve brown sugar
1 ½ cups mixed nuts
½ cup mixed seeds
Sea salt and black pepper to season
3 tbsp grated Parmesan cheese
½ tsp dried mixed herbs (oregano + thyme)

### Directions:

Preheat the oven to 350 F.

In a large bowl, beat the egg white, yeast extract, and swerve brown sugar. Add the mixed nuts and seeds; combine and spread onto a baking sheet. Bake in the oven for 10 minutes.

In a small bowl, mix the salt, black pepper, parmesan, and herbs.

Remove the nuts after and toss with the cheese mixture. Bake further for 5 minutes or until sticky and brown.

Transfer to a serving bowl; allow cooling for 5 minutes, and serve.

### Nutritional Fact per Serving:

Calories: 494; Fat: 48g; Total Carbs: 12g; Fiber: 6.2g; Net Carbs: 6.05g; Protein: 11g

# Chocolate Walnut Biscuits

These biscuits smell so good when they come out of the oven. Freshly baked biscuits with a walnut reveal that is definitely irresistible.

**PREPARATION TIME: 10 MINUTES • COOKING TIME: 20 MINUTES • SERVES: 4**

### Ingredients:

4 oz butter, softened
2 tbsp swerve sugar
2 tbsp swerve brown sugar
1 egg
1 tsp vanilla extract

½ cup almond flour
½ tsp baking soda
2/3 cup unsweetened chocolate chips
½ cup chopped walnuts

### Directions:

Preheat the oven to 350 F and lightly grease a baking sheet with cooking spray.

In a medium bowl, whisk the butter, swerve sugar, and swerve brown sugar until smooth. Beat in the egg and mix in the vanilla extract.

In another bowl, combine the almond flour with baking soda and mix into the wet ingredients. Fold in the chocolate chips and walnuts.

Spoon tablespoons full of the batter onto the baking sheet, creating 2-inch spaces in between each spoon, and press down each dough to slightly flatten.

Bake in the oven for 10 to 15 minutes or until cooked. Allow cooling in the oven for 5 minutes before transferring to a wire rack to cool completely. Serve.

### Nutritional Fact per Serving:

Calories: 430; Fat: 42.2g; Total Carbs: 7.9g; Fiber: 4.4g; Net Carbs: 3.5g; Protein: 6.3g

# Chocolate, Berries & Nuts Trail Mix Bars

I love this! Berries + chocolate + nuts and seeds is a power-packed snack item. Not much to say, just make them already and enjoy the love.

**PREPARATION TIME: 10 MINUTES • COOKING TIME: 15 MINUTES • SERVES: 4**

## Ingredients:

¼ cup walnuts
¼ cup cashew nuts
¼ cup almonds
¼ cup coconut chips
1 egg, beaten
½ cup butter, melted
¼ cup unsweetened dark chocolate chips
¼ cup mixed seeds
Salt to taste
1 cup mixed dried berries

## Directions:

Preheat the oven to 350 F and line a baking sheet with parchment paper.

In a food processor, pulse together the nuts for 1 to 2 minutes until roughly chopped.

Transfer to a large bowl and stir in the coconut chips, egg, butter, chocolate chips, mixed seeds, salt, and dried berries.

Spread the mixture in the baking sheet into an even layer and bake for 15 to 20 minutes or until golden brown.

Cool afterward and cut into bars.

## Nutritional Fact per Serving:

Calories: 384; Fat: 37.7g; Total Carbs: 9g; Fiber: 2.6g; Net Carbs: 6.4g; Protein: 6g

# STARTERS

## Chili Avocado with Cheese Sauce

Avocado is excellent greens when exploring different options. Spicing them and drizzling with some parmesan sauce is an excellent way to set the dinner table on bangers.

**PREPARATION TIME: 10 MINUTES • COOKING TIME: 6 MINUTES • SERVES: 4**

### Ingredients:

*For the cheese sauce:*

3 tbsp butter
3 tbsp almond flour
1 ½ cups almond milk
¼ tsp mustard powder
¼ tsp garlic powder

Black pepper to taste
1 cup grated cheddar cheese
4 oz cream cheese, softened
¼ cup grated Parmesan cheese

*For the chili avocado:*

2 large avocados, halved, pitted and sliced
2 tbsp melted butter

2 tbsp sriracha sauce
2 tbsp olive oil

### Directions:

*For the cheese sauce:*

Melt the butter in a medium saucepan, stir in the flour and cook until a golden. Whisk in the milk, mustard, garlic, and black pepper. Cook with continuous whisking until thickened, 2 minutes.

Stir in the cheddar cheese, cream cheese, and Parmesan cheese until melted.

*For the chili avocado:*

In a bowl, toss the avocado in the butter and hot sauce.

Heat the olive oil in a griddle pan over medium heat and cook in the avocado (in batches) until golden turning halfway, 3 to 4 minutes.

Plate the avocado and pour the cheese sauce all over. Serve immediately.

### Nutritional Fact per Serving:

Calories: 548; Fat: 49.2g; Total Carbs: 5.3g; Fiber: 2.1g; Net Carbs: 3.2g; Protein: 9.7g

# Goat Cheese and Raspberry Jam Focaccia Squares

These are pretty! Your guest will be curious to know what's following these treats. I love goat cheese for starts, they bring on such presence of flavors and gets everyone craving for more food.

**PREPARATION TIME: 5 MINUTES • COOKING TIME: 20 MINUTES • SERVES: 6**

## Ingredients:

*For the raspberry jam:*

1 cup fresh raspberries
2 cups erythritol

1 lemon, juiced

*For the focaccia squares:*

1 tbsp olive oil
1 cup cremini mushrooms, sliced
½ tsp dried thyme
Salt and black pepper to taste

6 low carb buns, cut into 4 squares each
2 oz goat cheese, crumbled
1 green onion, chopped

## Directions:

*For the raspberry jam:*

Pour the raspberries into a saucepan, break into a puree using a potato masher, and stir in the erythritol and lemon juice.

Place the pot over low heat and cook with constant stirring until the sugar dissolves. Turn the heat up to medium and allow the mixture boil for 4 minutes, still with constant stirring to prevent the jam from burning.

Turn the heat off after, allow cooling, and pour the mixture into sterilized jars.

*For the focaccia squares:*

Preheat the oven to 350 F.

Arrange the bread squares on a baking tray and place in the oven to warm for 7 to 10 minutes.

Meanwhile, heat the olive oil in a skillet over medium heat and sauté the mushrooms. Season with thyme, salt, and black pepper; cook until the mushrooms soften, 10 to 12 minutes.

Remove the bread squares from the oven, cut each square into halves horizontally, and divide the mushrooms on top. Share the cheese on top, some green onions, and raspberry jam. Cover with the other 6 pieces of focaccia. Serve immediately.

## Nutritional Fact per Serving:

Calories: 168; Fat: 12g; Total Carbs: 6.7g; Fiber: 1.6g; Net Carbs: 5.7g; Protein: 6.9g

# Chargrilled Broccoli in Tamarind-Peanut Sauce

That aroma from slightly burned vegetables is everything. I get tired of broccoli sautés sometimes, so this chargrilled version serves me well. I couldn't have thought of a better pair than peanut sauce.

**PREPARATION TIME: 15 MINUTES • COOKING TIME: 12 MINUTES • SERVES: 6**

## Ingredients:

### For the chargrilled broccoli:

2 cups water, for blanching
1 head broccoli, cut into florets
4 tbsp melted butter
1 small white onion, finely chopped

3 garlic cloves, minced
1 tsp dried basil
Salt and black pepper
A handful chopped parsley to garnish

### For the peanut sauce:

1 garlic clove, peeled
1 inch ginger, peeled
½ lemon, juiced
½ cup peanut butter

2 tbsp tamarind sauce
1 tsp swerve brown sugar
1 small red chili, chopped roughly
1/3 cup water

## Directions:

### For the chargrilled broccoli:

Simmer the water in a pot over medium heat and blanch the broccoli in the water for 2 minutes. Drain through a colander and pat dry with a paper towel.

In a medium bowl, mix the butter, onion, garlic, basil, salt, black pepper. Toss the broccoli florets in the mixture and allow marinating for 5 minutes.

Heat a grill pan over high heat and cook in the broccoli (in batches). When charred on one side, turn and cook the other side until charred too but not to burn.

Transfer to a plate and quickly make the peanut sauce while cooling.

### For the peanut sauce:

Place the garlic and ginger in a blender, turn on at medium speed, and blend until broken into pieces. Add the lemon juice, peanut butter, tamarind sauce, brown sugar, red chili, and water. Blend until smooth.

Serve the broccoli, pour the peanut sauce on top, toss, and garnish with parsley.

## Nutritional Fact per Serving:

Calories: 269; Fat: 18g; Total Carbs: 11g; Fiber: 5.6g; Net Carbs: 5.2g; Protein: 7.6g

# Tofu Skewers with Sesame Sauce

Could I have excluded tofu skewers? I love them any day, every day, and for every meal. These pair well with the sesame dipping sauce bring on so much flavor and taste to the tongue.

**PREPARATION TIME: 5 MINUTES • COOKING TIME: 8 MINUTES • SERVES: 4**

## Ingredients:

1 (14 oz) firm tofu
1 small zucchini, cut into 1-inch wedges
¼ cup cherry tomatoes, halved
1 small red onion, cut into wedges and separated

2 tbsp tahini + extra for serving
1 tbsp soy sauce
1 tbsp olive oil
Sesame seeds for garnishing

## Directions:

Place the tofu in between two paper towels and allow liquid draining for 5 minutes. After, cut the tofu into bite-size cubes.

In a bowl, mix the tahini and soy sauce, and toss the tofu in the sauce. Allow marinating for 15 to 30 minutes.

Thread the tofu, zucchini, cherry tomatoes and onion alternately on wooden skewers and set aside.

Heat the olive oil in a grill pan set over high heat until smoking and cook the tofu on both sides until golden brown, 6 to 8 minutes.

Plate the tofu skewers, garnish with sesame seeds, and serve with the some of the sesame dipping sauce.

## Nutritional Fact per Serving:

Calories: 266; Fat: 19g; Total Carbs: 6.3g; Fiber: 3.9g; Net Carbs: 2.4g; Protein: 14.9g

# Almond Cauliflower Cakes

A simple option for starting lunch. A little trick, when the main course is still cooking, serve these to reduce the hunger pang of the hungry family. Almond pairs well with cauliflower and creates a fantastic texture when used in cakes.

**PREPARATION TIME: 15 MINUTES • COOKING TIME: 8 MINUTES • SERVES: 4**

## Ingredients:

2 cups cauliflower florets
1 cup water for steaming
Salt and black pepper to taste

1 large egg, beaten
2 green onions, chopped
1 tbsp chopped parsley

½ cup grated Parmigiano Reggiano cheese
2 tbsp finely chopped almonds

1 cup golden flaxseed meal
1 cup olive oil

## Directions:

Pour the cauliflower and water into a medium pot and bring to a boil over medium heat until soft. Turn the heat off and drain through a colander. Transfer to a food processor and puree until very smooth. Pour into a bowl and mix in the salt, black pepper, egg, green onions, parsley, cheese, and almonds. Make 12 small cakes out of the mixture and coat in the flaxseed meal.

Heat the olive oil a deep frying pan and cook the patties on both sides until golden, 6 to 8 minutes. Use a slotted spoon to fetch onto a paper towel-lined plate. Serve warm with mayonnaise and lime wedges.

## Nutritional Fact per Serving:

Calories: 321; Fat: 23g; Total Carbs: 19g; Fiber: 13.3g; Net Carbs: 5.5g; Protein: 14.3g

# Roasted Green Pepper & Jalapeño Soup

Green peppers are my favorite vegetables. I use them sometimes when I need a little extra flavoring. So imagine what this soup turns out to be. Flavor certified, creaminess certified, and heat certified!

**PREPARATION TIME: 8 MINUTES • COOKING TIME: 30 MINUTES • SERVES: 4**

## Ingredients:

6 green bell peppers, halved and deseeded
1 jalapeño peppers, halved and deseeded
1 bulb garlic, halved but not peeled
6 tomatoes, halved
3 cups vegetable broth

Salt and black pepper to taste
2 tbsp melted butter
½ cup heavy cream
3 tbsp grated Parmesan cheese for topping
Roughly chopped chives to garnish

## Directions:

Preheat the oven to 350 F.

Arrange the bell peppers, jalapeño peppers, and garlic on a baking pan and roast for 15 minutes.

Add the tomatoes to the peppers and roast further for 15 minutes or until the vegetables char on the outside.

Take out the vegetables, allow cooling to handle, peel of the skins, and place in a blender. Add salt, black pepper, butter, and heavy cream; puree until completely smooth. Pour the soup into serving bowls, sprinkle with Parmesan cheese and chives, and serve.

## Nutritional Fact per Serving:

Calories: 189; Fat: 12g; Total Carbs: 12.2g; Fiber: 3.5g; Net Carbs: 8.7g; Protein: 5.3g

# Crostini with Vegan Bacon and Avocado

As simple as life can get, toast some low carb bread, create an avocado paté, and load it up with cheese, nuts, and vegan bacon. Wouldn't you rather try this soon?

**PREPARATION TIME: 5 MINUTES • COOKING TIME: 20 MINUTES • SERVES: 4**

## Ingredients:

2 tbsp + 2 tbsp olive oil + extra for topping
2 avocados, halved and pitted
¼ tsp garlic powder
¼ tsp onion powder
Salt and black pepper to taste
1 tbsp chopped parsley
1 lemon, zested and juiced
1 loaf low carb bread, sliced into 2-inch pieces
2 garlic cloves, peeled and halved
3 tbsp grated Parmesan cheese
2 tbsp chopped toasted pecans

## Directions:

In a bowl, using a fork, mix the 2 tbsp of olive oil, avocado flesh, garlic powder, onion powder, salt, black pepper, parsley, lemon zest, and juice until smooth and evenly combined. Set aside.

Heat a grill pan over high heat, meanwhile; rub both sides of the bread slices with garlic and brush with the remaining olive oil. Grill the bread on both sides in the heated pan until crispy and golden brown.

Transfer crostini to a plate and spread generously with the avocado mixture. Sprinkle with Parmesan cheese and some pecans. Drizzle with some more olive oil and serve.

## Nutritional Fact per Serving:

Calories: 327; Fat: 31.9g; Total Carbs: 11g; Fiber: 7.2g; Net Carbs: 3.9g; Protein: 3.6g

# SIDE DISHES

## Speedy Slaw with Pecans

And here, you have your delicious slaw on the keto diet. This recipe is perfect and the slaw tastes better than any out there, thanks to the pecans.

**PREPARATION TIME: 20 MINUTES • SERVES: 4**

### Ingredients:

2 cups packaged broccoli slaw
1 (sweet) red bell pepper, deseeded and thinly sliced
1 medium red onion, thinly sliced
2 tbsp chopped cilantro
Salt and black pepper to taste
A handful of toasted pecans, chopped
2 tbsp flax seeds
1 tbsp red wine vinegar
2 tbsp olive oil
½ lemon, juiced
1 tsp Dijon mustard
2 tbsp mayonnaise

### Directions:

In a bowl, combine the broccoli slaw, bell pepper, red onion, cilantro, and season with salt and black pepper. Mix in the pecans and flax seeds.

In a small bowl, whisk the red wine vinegar, olive oil, lemon juice, mayonnaise, and Dijon mustard. Drizzle the dressing over the slaw and mix.

Serve immediately or chilled with grilled tempeh and buttered mushrooms.

### Nutritional Fact per Serving:

Calories: 310; Fat: 31.2g; Total Carbs: 7.2g; Fiber: 3.9g; Net Carbs: 3.2g; Protein: 4.8g

# Walnut Roasted Asparagus

Yup! I dared things a bit. And it worked. Roasted asparagus are basic, but cooking them with some walnuts, add on that extra feel for your main dishes. In short, the aroma is massively improved this way.

**PREPARATION TIME: 5 MINUTES • COOKING TIME: 12 MINUTES • SERVES: 4**

## Ingredients:

*For the asparagus:*

2 tbsp olive oil
1 garlic clove, crushed
1 tbsp tamarind sauce

A handful of walnuts, roughly chopped
1 ¼ lb asparagus, trimmed

*For the dressing:*

3 tbsp tahini
2 tbsp balsamic vinegar

½ tbsp red chili pepper, chopped

## Directions:

Preheat the oven to 350 F.

In a bowl, mix the olive oil, garlic, tamarind sauce, and walnuts.

Lay the asparagus on a baking tray and drizzle the tamarind mixture all over. Toss the vegetables to properly coat and roast in the oven until tender and charred lightly, 10 to 12 minutes.

Meanwhile, in a bowl, whisk the tahini, balsamic vinegar, and chili pepper. Plate the asparagus when ready, drizzle with the dressing, and serve with fried tofu cubes.

## Nutritional Fact per Serving:

Calories: 359; Fat: 32g; Total Carbs: 14.5 g; Fiber: 6.1g; Net Carbs: 8.4g; Protein: 9.6g

# Cheesy Zucchini Bake

For fresh salads, grilled tempeh and tofu, this cheesy zucchini dish will pair up nicely. It is delicious, but quickly satisfying. You may be digging more and more into the casserole. Watch out!

**PREPARATION TIME: 10 MINUTES • COOKING TIME: 15 MINUTES • SERVES: 4**

## Ingredients:

3 large zucchinis, thinly sliced
3 tbsp salted butter, melted
2 tbsp olive oil
1 garlic clove, minced

1 tsp dried thyme
¼ cup grated mozzarella cheese
2/3 cup grated Parmesan cheese

## Directions:

Preheat the oven to 350 F.

Arrange the zucchini in a large colander and sprinkle with salt. Allow liquid draining for 5 to 7 minutes and then, pat the zucchini slices dry with a paper towel.

Pour the vegetables in a bowl; add the butter, olive oil, garlic, and thyme. Toss until the zucchini properly coat with the oil and spice.

Spread into a baking dish and sprinkle with the mozzarella and Parmesan cheese. Bake in the oven for 15 minutes or until the cheese melts and is golden.

Remove from the oven and serve warm with garden green salad.

## Nutritional Fact per Serving:

Calories: 194; Fat: 17.2g; Total Carbs: 3.2g; Fiber: 0.3g; Net Carbs: 3g; Protein: 7.4g

# Tofu and Mushroom Kebabs

The inspiration is for this option is my naughty character of picking loaded skewers at parties. So, when there's the option to be creative, I combine mushrooms, tofu, and onion on single sticks. The aim was to add more, but some consideration is pardoned. Enjoy!

**PREPARATION TIME: 12 MINUTES • COOKING TIME: 20 MINUTES • SERVES: 2**

## Ingredients:

1 (14 oz) block extra firm tofu
1 cup white button mushrooms, quartered
2 small red onions, cut into wedges
8 wooden skewers

2 tbsp olive oil
1 tsp Chinese five-spice
1 lemon, juiced
2 tbsp chopped parsley, to garnish

## Directions:

Place the tofu between two paper towels and allow soaking for 5 minutes. Cut the tofu into bite-size cubes.

Thread the tofu, mushrooms, and onions alternately on the skewers and set aside.

In a bowl, mix the olive oil, Chinese five-spice, and lemon juice. Brush the vegetable skewers with the sauce.

Cook in a grill pan over high heat until the vegetables soften and lightly char.

Transfer to a plate, garnish with parsley, and serve with garlic cauli rice and steamed broccoli.

## Nutritional Fact per Serving:

Calories: 372; Fat: 27g; Total Carbs: 9.7g; Fiber: 2.8g; Net Carbs: 6.9g; Protein: 25g

# Almond Bread and Vegan Bacon Pudding

You bet this should be for breakfast! But, the combination makes it more lunch worthy. Serve with sautéed vegetables and some hot sauce drizzle. You will love it!

**PREPARATION TIME: 10 MINUTES • COOKING TIME: 25 MINUTES • SERVES: 4**

## Ingredients:

1 tbsp olive oil
3 vegan bacon slices, chopped
1 orange bell pepper, deseeded and chopped
3 tbsp unsalted butter, softened
6 slices low carb bread

1 small red onion, finely chopped
3 eggs
1 ½ cup almond milk
3 tbsp grated cheddar cheese
2 tbsp grated parmesan cheese

## Directions:

Preheat the oven to 300 F.

Heat the oil in a skillet over medium heat; add the vegan bacon and bell pepper. Cook until the bacon browns and the bell pepper softens.

Meanwhile, brush a baking dish with the butter and apply some on both sides of each bread slice. Cut into cubes and arrange in the baking dish. Scatter with the onions, vegan bacon, and bell pepper.

In a bowl, beat the eggs with milk and pour the mixture over. Sprinkle with the cheddar and Parmesan cheeses and bake the ingredients in the oven for 20 minutes or until golden on top.

Serve afterward.

## Nutritional Fact per Serving:

Calories: 362; Fat: 27g; Total Carbs: 13g; Fiber: 4.8g; Net Carbs: 7.7g; Protein: 13.3g

# Chili Broccoli Rabe with Sesame Seeds

Broccoli rabe cooks soft with a little bit of crunch, some heat, and sesame seeds to add some extra crunch. Serve with cauli rice, tofu meatballs, and many main dishes.

**PREPARATION TIME: 8 MINUTES • COOKING TIME: 4 MINUTES • SERVES: 4**

## Ingredients:

3 cups broccoli rabe, chopped roughly
1 cup water
1 tbsp melted butter
1 tbsp olive oil
1 garlic clove, minced

1 orange bell pepper, deseeded and sliced
Salt and black pepper to taste
Red chili flakes, for garnishing

## Directions:

Cook the broccoli rabe in lightly salted water over medium heat for 2 to 3 minutes or until softened. Drain well after in a colander.

Heat the butter and olive oil in a wide skillet and sauté the garlic and bell pepper until fragrant and softened.

Toss in the broccoli and cook for 1 minute or until heated up.

Pour into a serving bowl, sprinkle with some chilies, and serve warm pan-fried cauliflower meatballs.

## Nutritional Fact per Serving:

Calories: 68; Fat: 6.4g; Total Carbs: 2.1g; Fiber: 1g; Net Carbs: 1.1g; Protein: 1.2g

# Saffron Cauli Rice with Fried Garlic

I cooked this option for my best friend recently; we served it with some leftover stew and it rocked. Saffron and garlic a good combination for flavoring, meanwhile saffron gives the rice a pretty yellow color and the fried garlic, an intense flavor and crunch as you chew.

**PREPARATION TIME: 14 MINUTES • COOKING TIME: 20 MINUTES • SERVES: 4**

## Ingredients:

1 tbsp olive oil
6 garlic cloves, thinly sliced
1 tbsp butter
1 small yellow onion, thinly sliced
2 cups cauli rice

A pinch of saffron soaked in ¼-cup almond milk
¼ cup vegetable broth
Salt and black pepper to taste
2 tbsp chopped parsley

## Directions:

Heat the olive oil in a medium pot and fry in the garlic until golden brown but not burned. Remove with a slotted spoon onto a paper towel-lined plate. Set aside.

Add the butter to the oil and sauté the onion for 3 minutes. Stir in the cauli rice; remove the saffron from the milk and pour the milk and vegetable stock into the pot. Mix, cover the pot, and cook for 5 minutes or until the cauli rice is soft but not mushy.

Turn the heat, season with salt, black pepper, and add the parsley. Fluff the rice and dish into serving plates. Garnish with the fried garlic and serve with stewed tofu.

## Nutritional Fact per Serving:

Calories: 91; Fat: 6.6g; Total Carbs: 7.5g; Fiber: 1.6g; Net Carbs: 5.9g; Protein: 1.69g

# One-Pan Mixed Garden Greens

Instead of having your greens in a salad, toss them in some red wine vinegar, butter, spices, and nuts. Your taste buds will be attracted.

**PREPARATION TIME: 15 MINUTES • COOKING TIME: 8 MINUTES • SERVES: 4**

## Ingredients:

1 small red onion, finely sliced
A pinch swerve sugar
2 tbsp red wine vinegar
2 tbsp butter
1 tsp cumin powder
1 garlic clove, minced

1 cup asparagus, trimmed and chopped
2 cups mixed garden greens
4 tbsp chopped parsley
Olive oil for drizzling
A handful pine nuts

## Directions:

In a small bowl, whisk the onion, swerve sugar and vinegar evenly and set aside.

Melt the butter in a skillet over medium heat and stir in the cumin and garlic. Cook for 1 to 2 minutes or until fragrant.

Add the asparagus and allow softening for 5 minutes. Put in the mixed garden greens and mix. Reduce the heat to low and steam the vegetables for 1 minute.

Turn the heat off and stir in the parsley.

Plate the food, drizzle with plenty of olive oil, and garnish with pine nuts. Serve immediately with grilled zucchini and hot sauce.

## Nutritional Fact per Serving:

Calories: 79; Fat: 6.18g; Total Carbs: 5.06g; Fiber: 1.5g; Net Carbs: 3.5g; Protein: 1.9g

# Walnuts Broccoli Rice

An excellent way to infuse some nuts into regular broccoli rice. Walnuts create solid textures to chew on while sharing its portion of flavors and tastes to the dish. The dish serves well with sauces, grills, and mixed vegetables.

**PREPARATION TIME: 15 MINUTES • COOKING TIME: 10 MINUTES • SERVES: 4**

## Ingredients:

2 tbsp butter
1 garlic clove, minced
2 heads large broccoli, riced
½ cup vegetable broth

Salt and black pepper to taste
¼ cup toasted walnuts, chopped
4 tbsp sesame seeds, toasted
3 tbsp chopped cilantro

## Directions:

Melt the butter in a pot over medium heat and stir in the garlic. Cook until fragrant, for a minute and stir in the broccoli and vegetable broth. Allow steaming for 2 minutes. Season with salt and black pepper and cook covered for 3 to 5 minutes or until the softened but not mushy.

Open the lid; pour in the walnuts, sesame seeds, and cilantro. Fluff the rice and adjust the taste with salt and black pepper as desired. Plate the rice and serve with coconut tempeh stir-fry.

## Nutritional Fact per Serving:

Calories: 240; Fat: 15g; Total Carbs: 12.2g; Fiber: 9.2g; Net Carbs: 3g; Protein: 11g

# Cheese Bread

Bread on the keto diet could be a tough decision, so how about you bake yours and load it with plenty of cheese while using almond flour. The outcome is a tastier, fuller, and richer loaf that the bakery wouldn't offer.

**PREPARATION TIME: 13 MINUTES • COOKING TIME: 45 MINUTES • SERVES: 4**

## Ingredients:

1 tbsp almond flour
8 tbsp butter
2 medium white onions, chopped
1 cup ricotta cheese

1 cup grated cheddar cheese
1 cup almond meal
1 cup almond milk
6 eggs, separated

## Directions:

Preheat the oven to 350 F, lightly grease a 10 x 13 inch baking tin with cooking spray, and sprinkle with almond flour. Shake to stick the flour to the oil and pour out the excess. Set aside.

Melt 1 tbsp of butter in a frying pan over medium heat and sauté the onions until softened. Turn the heat off and set aside.

In a bowl, with an electric mixer, beat the remaining butter with ricotta cheese until smooth. Add the cheddar cheese and cooked onions. Mix again.

In a separate bowl, thoroughly mix the almond meal and milk and pour the mixture into the cheese batter. Combine evenly and pour the mixture into the baking tin.

Shake to level the mixture and place in the oven to bake for 45 minutes or until a skewer inserted into the bread comes out clean.

Take out the tin, remove the bread onto a wire rack to cool for 5 minutes, slice, and serve with creamy mushroom soup.

## Nutritional Fact per Serving:

Calories: 508; Fat: 40.8g; Total Carbs: 8.g; Fiber: 2.3g; Net Carbs: 5.7g; Protein: 20.2g

# Broccoli and Lettuce Soup with Poached Eggs

This soup will set you off for a good evening when not up for a heavy meal. The greenly color whets the appetite and the egg topping creates sumptuous swallows.

**PREPARATION TIME: 10 MINUTES • COOKING TIME: 30 MINUTES • SERVES: 4**

## Ingredients:

1 tbsp olive oil
2 tbsp butter
1 medium red onion, thinly sliced
3 garlic cloves, finely sliced
1 large head broccoli, cut into florets
1 medium lettuce head, leaves extracted and chopped

4 cups vegetable stock
6 sprigs parsley, leaves extracted
Salt and black pepper to taste
1 tbsp fresh dill leaves for garnishing
1 cup water
4 eggs
1 cup grated Parmesan cheese for topping

## Directions:

Melt the oil and butter in a large saucepan over medium heat and sauté the onion and garlic until softened and fragrant, 3 minutes.

Stir in the broccoli and lettuce and cook until the lettuce wilts.

Pour in the vegetable stock, parsley and season with salt and black pepper. Cover the pot and bring the ingredients to a boil. Reduce the heat and simmer for 10 minutes or until the broccoli softens.

Open the lid and use an immersion blender to puree the soup until completely smooth. Adjust the taste with salt and black pepper.

Meanwhile, bring the water to a boil in a large saucepan over medium heat. Create a whirlpool in the center of the water using a wooden spoon. After, allow the water to almost settle back to normal and crack in an egg. Poach for 3 minutes, remove with a slotted spoon, and set aside in a plate. Repeat poaching the remaining eggs.

Divide the soup into serving bowls, top with a poached egg each, garnish with some dill leaves, Parmesan cheese, and serve warm.

## Nutritional Fact per Serving:

Calories: 515; Fat: 33.9g; Total Carbs: 9.1g; Fiber: 4.6g; Net Carbs: 4.5g; Protein: 38.3g

# Creamy Mushroom Tofu Soup

Recall the tofu mushroom skewers? Here's another way to combine similar ingredients into something lighter and creamier. Instead, I use silken tofu instead of firm tofu to help create that creamy consistency that I desired.

**PREPARATION TIME: 10 MINUTES • COOKING TIME: 18 MINUTES • SERVES: 4**

## Ingredients:

1 tbsp olive oil
1 garlic clove, minced
1 large white onion, finely chopped
1 tsp ginger puree
1 cup vegetable stock
2 turnips, peeled and chopped
Salt and black pepper to taste
2 (14 oz) silken tofu, drained and rinsed
2/3 cup cremini mushrooms, sliced and pre-cooked
2 cups almond milk
1 tbsp chopped basil
Finely chopped parsley to garnish
Chopped walnuts for topping

## Directions:

Heat the olive oil in a saucepan and sauté the garlic, onion, and ginger puree until fragrant and soft.

Pour in the vegetable stock, turnip, season with salt, and black pepper. Cook until the turnips soften, 6 minutes. Add the silken tofu and use an immersion blender to puree the ingredients until very smooth.

Stir in the mushrooms and simmer covered for 7 minutes or until the mushrooms heat up making sure the tofu doesn't curdle up.

Add the milk and heat for 2 minutes and taste and adjust the taste with salt and black pepper. Stir in the basil and dish the soup into serving bowls.

Garnish with parsley and serve with soy chorizo chips.

## Nutritional Fact per Serving:

Calories: 923; Fat: 8.5g; Total Carbs: 12g; Fiber: 4.8g; Net Carbs: 7.4g; Protein: 23.4g

# Creamy Onion Soup

French onion soup is one of my favorite's to chill with when having an easy day. To make it keto perfect, I added some almond milk and cheese for that creamy goodness.

**PREPARATION TIME: 10 MINUTES • COOKING TIME: 65 MINUTES • SERVES: 4**

## Ingredients:

2 tbsp butter
1 tbsp olive oil
3 cups thinly sliced white onions
2 garlic cloves, thinly sliced
2 tsp almond flour
½ cup dry white wine

Salt and black pepper to taste
2 sprigs chopped rosemary
2 cups hot water
2 cups almond milk
1 cup grates Parmesan cheese

## Directions:

Heat the butter and oil in a pot over medium heat. Sauté the onions for 10 minutes or until softened, stirring regularly to avoid browning. Reduce the heat to low and cook further for 15 minutes, stirring occasionally.

Add the garlic, cook further for 10 minutes or until the onions caramelize while still stirring.

Stir in the flour well, add the wine, and increase the heat. Season with salt, black pepper, rosemary, and pour in the hot water. Cover the pot, and bring to a boil, then simmer for 30 minutes.

Pour in the milk and half of the cheese. Stir to melt the cheese, adjust the taste with salt, black pepper, and spoon the soup into a serving bowl. Top with more Parmesan cheese and serve.

## Nutritional Fact per Serving:

Calories: 340; Fat: 23.4g; Total Carbs: 7.2g; Fiber: 1.6g; Net Carbs: 5.6g; Protein: 15.1g

# Spring Vegetable Soup

I never used to make spring vegetables into a soup. I will often roast them and eat with some grilled tofu. After trying this, I got re-wired. It is delicious!

**PREPARATION TIME: 8 MINUTES • COOKING TIME: 15 MINUTES • SERVES: 4**

## Ingredients:

4 cups vegetable stock
1 cup pearl onions, peeled and halved
3 cups green beans, chopped
2 cups asparagus, chopped

2 cups baby spinach
1 tbsp garlic powder
Salt and freshly ground white pepper to taste
2 cups grated Parmesan cheese, for serving

## Directions:

Pour the vegetable broth into a pot; add the pearl onions, green beans, and asparagus. Season with garlic powder, salt and white pepper, cover the pot, and simmer for 10 minutes or until the asparagus softens.

Stir in the spinach and allow slight wilting. Adjust the taste with salt and white pepper.

Dish into serving bowls and top with plenty Parmesan cheese. Serve with low carb bread.

## Nutritional Fact per Serving:

Calories: 196; Fat: 11.9g; Total Carbs: 10g; Fiber: 5.7g; Net Carbs: 4.3g; Protein: 2.5g

# Ginger - Spinach & Poached Egg Soup

Poached eggs are the item of feature in this soup. They offer some weight to creamy green soup, which I find to be a new touch.

**PREPARATION TIME: 8 MINUTES • COOKING TIME: 13 MINUTES • SERVES: 4**

## Ingredients:

1 tbsp butter
1 tbsp sesame oil + extra for drizzling
1 small onion, finely sliced
3 garlic cloves, minced
2 tsp ginger paste
2 cups baby spinach, chopped
2 cups chopped green beans
4 cups vegetable stock
3 tbsp chopped cilantro + extra for garnish
Salt and black pepper to taste
3 cups water
4 eggs

## Directions:

Melt the butter with the sesame oil in a large pot over medium heat. Sauté the onions and garlic until fragrant and soft, 3 minutes. Add the ginger and cook for 2 minutes, stirring frequently.

Stir in the spinach, allowing wilting, and pour in the green beans, stock, and cilantro. Season with salt and black pepper. Cover the pot and bring to boil, reduce the heat, and simmer for 7 to 10 minutes or until slightly thickened.

Meanwhile, bring the water to simmer and when hot, crack the eggs into the water to poach for 3 minutes. Use a slotted spoon to remove the eggs onto a paper towel-lined plate and set aside.

Turn the heat off under the soup and pour the ingredients into a blender. Puree the content until very smooth and share into four serving bowls. Adjust the taste with salt and black pepper.

Place an egg on each soup, drizzle with extra sesame oil, some cilantro, and serve.

## Nutritional Fact per Serving:

Calories: 463; Fat: 30g; Total Carbs: 8.5g; Fiber: 2.7g; Net Carbs: 5.8g; Protein: 23.6g

# Parsnip – Tomato Soup

Rather simple, but nutritious. Cook some parsnips and tomatoes in butter, spices, and coconut milk. Blend smoothly and top generously with walnuts and parmesan cheese. That makes a classic!

**PREPARATION TIME: 5 MINUTES • COOKING TIME: 28 MINUTES • SERVES: 4**

## Ingredients:

1 tbsp butter
1 tbsp olive oil
1 large red onion, chopped
4 garlic cloves, minced
6 red bell peppers, deseeded and sliced
1 daikon radish, peeled and chopped
2 parsnips, peeled and chopped

3 cups chopped tomatoes
4 cups vegetable stock
Salt and black pepper to taste
3 cups coconut milk
2 cups toasted chopped walnuts
1 cup grated Parmesan cheese

## Directions:

Heat the butter and olive oil in a medium pot over medium heat; sauté the onion and garlic until fragrant and soft, 3 minutes.

Stir in the red bell peppers, daikon radish, and parsnips; cook for 10 minutes until sweaty. Pour in the tomatoes, vegetable stock, salt, and black pepper. Cover the lid and simmer for 20 minutes.

Turn the heat off and puree the ingredients with an immersion blender. Add the coconut milk, season with black pepper, and blitz a few more times until evenly mixed.

Pour the soup into serving bowls and garnish generously with walnuts and Parmesan cheese.

## Nutritional Fact per Serving:

Calories: 955; Fat: 86.6g; Total Carbs: 10.5g; Fiber: 6.5g; Net Carbs: 4g; Protein: 19.1g

# Chilled Lemongrass and Avocado Soup

Are you looking for something sweet for lunch or dinner? Here, you have something worth every bit of your efforts. Remember to chill the soup before enjoying.

**PREPARATION TIME: 5 MINUTES • COOKING TIME: 15 MINUTES • SERVES: 4**

## Ingredients:

4 cups chopped avocado pulp
2 stalks lemongrass, chopped
4 cups vegetable broth
2 lemons, juiced

3 tbsp chopped mint + extra to garnish
Salt and black pepper to taste
2 cups heavy cream

## Directions:

Bring the avocado, lemongrass, and vegetable broth to a slow boil in a large pot over low heat to soften the lemongrass and warm the avocado.

Add the lemon juice, mint, salt, pepper, and puree the ingredients using an immersion blender. Stir in the heavy cream and turn the heat off. Spoon into serving bowls and chill for 1 hour. Garnish with some extra mint and serve the soup.

## Nutritional Fact per Serving:

Calories: 339; Fat: 33.3g; Total Carbs: 6.5g; Fiber: 3g; Net Carbs: 3.5g; Protein: 3.5g

# Herby Cheese Soup

When soups include a special touch, I find myself there. Like in this recipe, the soup features a play of herbs, which balance off with the texture of coconut flour and almond milk. It will make a good impression.

**PREPARATION TIME: 12 MINUTES • COOKING TIME: 10 MINUTES • SERVES: 4**

## Ingredients:

1 tbsp olive oil
6 slices vegan bacon, chopped
4 tbsp butter
1 small white onion, roughly chopped
3 garlic cloves, minced
2 tbsp finely chopped thyme
1 tbsp chopped fresh tarragon

1 tbsp chopped fresh oregano
2 cups peeled and cubed parsnips
3 ½ cups vegetable broth
Salt and black pepper to taste
1 cup almond milk
1 cup grated cheddar cheese
2 tbsp chopped scallions for garnishing

## Directions:

Heat the olive oil in a skillet over medium heat and fry the vegan bacon until browned and crunchy, 5 minutes. Spoon onto a paper towel-lined plate and set aside.

Melt the butter in a large saucepan over medium heat. Sauté the onion, garlic, thyme, tarragon, and oregano until softened and fragrant.

Add the parsnips, season with salt and black pepper, and cook for 10 to 12 minutes or until the parsnips soften.

Using an immersion blender, process the soup until very smooth. Stir in the milk and cheese and simmer with continuous stirring until the cheese melts.

Divide the mixture into four soup bowls, share the vegan bacon on top, and garnish with scallions.

## Nutritional Fact per Serving:

Calories: 775; Fat: 57.4g; Total Carbs: 8.6g; Fiber: 2.1g; Net Carbs: 6.5g; Protein: 18.2g

# Cherry Tomato Salad with Soy Chorizo

When I was non-vegetarian, chorizo happened to my most loved. Finding soy chorizo meant a lot to me, so when making some cherry tomato salad, it doesn't hurt to add some soy chorizo.

**PREPARATION TIME: 5 MINUTES • COOKING TIME: 5 MINUTES • SERVES: 4**

## Ingredients:

2 ½ tbsp olive oil
4 soy chorizo sausages, chopped
2 tsp red wine vinegar
1 small red onion, finely chopped

2 ½ cups cherry tomatoes, halved
2 tbsp chopped cilantro
Salt and black pepper to taste
Sliced Kalamata olives to garnish

## Directions:

Heat half tablespoon of olive oil in a skillet and fry the soy chorizo until golden. Turn heat off.

In a salad bowl, whisk the remaining olive oil with the red wine vinegar and add the onion, cherry tomatoes, cilantro, and soy chorizo. Mix to evenly coat in the dressing; season with salt and black pepper.

Garnish with the olives and serve.

## Nutritional Fact per Serving:

Calories: 138; Fat: 8.9g; Total Carbs: 5.6g; Fiber: 0.4g; Net Carbs: 5.2g; Protein: 7.1g

# Buttered Greens with Almonds and Tofu Salad

Loaded nourishment with a play of my favorite keto-vegetarian elements.

**PREPARATION TIME: 10 MINUTES • COOKING TIME: 15 MINUTES • SERVES: 4**

## Ingredients:

2 tbsp olive oil
1 (7 oz) block pack extra firm tofu
2 tbsp butter
1 cup green beans, trimmed

1 cup asparagus, trimmed and halved
Salt and black pepper to taste
½ lemon, juiced
4 tbsp chopped almonds

## Directions:

Place the tofu in between two paper towels and allow draining for 5 minutes. After, remove the napkins and chop into small cubes.

Heat the olive oil in a skillet and fry the tofu until golden, 10 minutes. Remove onto a paper towel-lined plate and set aside.

Add the butter to the skillet to melt and pour in the green beans and asparagus; season with salt and black pepper, toss and cook until softened. Mix in the tofu and stir-fry further for 5 minutes.

Transfer to serving plates, drizzle with lemon juice, and scatter the almonds on top.

Serve warm to a side of egg cauliflower fried rice.

## Nutritional Fact per Serving:
Calories: 237; Fat: 19.5g; Total Carbs: 5.9g; Fiber: 2.1g; Net Carbs: 3.9; Protein: 12.7g

# Roasted Bell Pepper Salad with Olives

Roast some red bell pepper, combine with some olives, and balsamic vinegar and watch how your body's system gets igniting. It is a simple salad, but yet delicious.

**PREPARATION TIME: 10 MINUTES • COOKING TIME: 20 MINUTES • SERVES: 4**

## Ingredients:
8 large red bell peppers, deseeded and cut in wedges
½ tsp swerve sugar
2 ½ tbsp olive oil
1/3 cup arugula
1/3 cup pitted Kalamata olives
1 tbsp mint leaves
3 tbsp toasted chopped walnuts
½ tbsp balsamic vinegar
Crumbled goat cheese for topping
Toasted pine nuts for topping

## Directions:
Preheat the oven to 400 F.

Pour the bell peppers on a roasting pan; season with the swerve sugar and drizzle with half of the olive oil. Roast in the oven for 20 minutes or until slightly charred; remove from the oven and set aside to cool.

Arrange the arugula in a salad bowl and scatter with the roasted bell peppers, olives, mint leaves, walnuts, and drizzle with the balsamic vinegar and remaining olive oil. Season with salt and black pepper.

Toss; top with the goat cheese and pine nuts and serve.

## Nutritional Fact per Serving:
Calories: 163; Fat: 13.3g; Total Carbs: 6.5g; Fiber: 2.2g; Net Carbs: 4.3g; Protein: 3.3g

# Grandma's Cauliflower Salad with Peanuts

The first time I tried this salad, I loved it and that's why I added it to this collection. This is a good blend of little carbs with many fatty elements. It will serve your dieting needs well.

**PREPARATION TIME: 8 MINUTES • COOKING TIME: 10 MINUTES • SERVES: 4**

## Ingredients:

1 small head cauliflower, cut into florets
12 green olives, pitted and roughly chopped
8 sun-dried tomatoes in olive oil, drained
3 tbsp chopped scallions
1 lemon, zested and juiced
2 tbsp sesame oil

A handful of toasted peanuts
3 tbsp chopped parsley
½ cup watercress
Salt and black pepper to taste
Lemon wedges to garnish

## Directions:

Bring the water to a boil in a medium pot over medium heat. Pour the cauliflower into a steamer basket and soften over the boiling water, 10 minutes. Turn the heat off and transfer the cauliflower to a large salad bowl.

Add the olives, sun-dried tomatoes, scallions, lemon zest and juice, sesame oil, peanuts, parsley, and watercress. Season with salt, black pepper, and mix using a ladle. Allow slight cooling and serve with lemon wedges.

## Nutritional Fact per Serving:

Calories: 203; Fat: 15.2g; Total Carbs: 9.6g; Fiber: 3.2g; Net Carbs: 6.4g; Protein: 6.6g

# Roasted Asparagus with Goat Cheese and Cilantro

Give your asparagus some life with some roasting and blending with hazelnuts, goat cheese, and cilantro for intense flavor. It is a beauty!

**PREPARATION TIME: 10 MINUTES • COOKING TIME: 20 MINUTES • SERVES: 4**

## Ingredients:

1 lb asparagus, trimmed and halved
2 tbsp olive oil
½ tsp dried tarragon
½ tsp dried oregano
Salt and black pepper to taste
½ tsp sesame seeds
1 tbsp maple (sugar-free) syrup

½ cup arugula
4 tbsp crumbled goat cheese
2 tbsp hazelnuts
1 lemon, cut into wedges

## Directions:

Preheat the oven to 350 F.

Pour the asparagus on a baking tray, drizzle with the olive oil, tarragon, oregano, salt, black pepper, and sesame seeds. Toss with your hands and roast in the oven for 15 minutes; remove and drizzle the maple syrup, and continue cooking for 5 minutes or until slightly charred.

Spread the arugula in a large salad bowl and spoon the asparagus on top. Scatter with the goat cheese, hazelnuts, and serve with the lemon wedges.

## Nutritional Fact per Serving:

Calories: 146; Fat: 12.9g; Total Carbs: 5g; Fiber: 1.6g; Net Carbs: 3.4g; Protein: 4.4g

# Warm Mushroom and Yellow Pepper Salad

Sounds simple to make, but tastes a million thanks to the blend of simple spices and soy sauce. Enjoying the salad warm created that extra touch from a chilled salad.

**PREPARATION TIME: 15 MINUTES • COOKING TIME: 5 MINUTES • SERVES: 4**

## Ingredients:

2 tbsp sesame oil
2 yellow bell peppers, deseeded and finely sliced
1 cup mixed mushrooms, chopped
1 garlic clove, minced
2 tbsp tamarind sauce
½ tsp hot sauce
1 tsp maple (sugar-free) syrup
½ tsp ginger paste
Chopped toasted pecans for topping
Sesame seeds to garnish

## Directions:

Heat half of the sesame oil in a large skillet, sauté the bell peppers and mushrooms until slightly softened, 8 to 10 minutes.

In a bowl, mix the garlic, tamarind sauce, hot sauce, maple syrup, and ginger paste. Stir the mix into the vegetables and stir-fry for 2 to 3 minutes.

Turn the heat off and divide the salad onto four plates; drizzle with the remaining sesame oil and garnish with pecans and sesame seeds. Serve with grilled tofu.

## Nutritional Fact per Serving:

Calories: 289; Fat: 26.7g; Total Carbs: 9g; Fiber: 3.8g; Net Carbs: 5.2g; Protein: 4.2g

# Broccoli, Spinach, and Feta Salad

Feta cheese is one of my favorites cheeses and yet unique in nature. It tastes good in salad and this did not disappoint. You want to try this soon.

**PREPARATION TIME: 15 MINUTES • SERVES: 4**

## Ingredients:

2 tbsp olive oil
1 tbsp white wine vinegar
2 tbsp poppy seeds
Salt and black pepper to taste
2 cups broccoli slaw

2 cups chopped spinach
1/3 cup chopped walnuts
1/3 cup sunflower seeds
1/3 cup blueberries
2/3 cup chopped feta cheese

## Directions:

In a small bowl, whisk the olive oil, white wine vinegar, poppy seeds, salt, and pepper. Set aside. In a large salad bowl, combine the broccoli slaw, spinach, walnuts, sunflower seeds, blueberries, and feta cheese. Drizzle the dressing on top, toss, and serve.

## Nutritional Fact per Serving:

Calories: 397; Fat: 3.87g; Total Carbs: 8.4g; Fiber: 3.5g; Net Carbs: 4.9g; Protein: 8.9g

# Zucchini and Dill Bowls with Goat-Feta Cheese

Balancing its way between a main course and salad, you can enjoy this dish whichever way. The goal is to have a generous amount of goat and feta cheese for that extra touch.

**PREPARATION TIME: 10 MINUTES • COOKING TIME: 25 MINUTES • SERVES: 4**

## Ingredients:

4 zucchinis, spiralized and cut roughly
Salt and black pepper to taste
½ lemon, zested and 1 tbsp juice
1 tbsp olive oil
¼ tsp Dijon mustard

1 tbsp freshly chopped dill leaves
½ cup baby kale
1/3 cup crumbled goat cheese
1/3 cup crumbled feta cheese
2 tbsp toasted pine nuts

## Directions:

Put the zucchinis in a medium bowl and season with salt and pepper. In a small bowl, mix the lemon juice, olive oil, and Dijon mustard. Pour the mixture over the zucchini and toss evenly. Add the dill, kale, goat cheese, feta cheese, and pine nuts. Toss with two ladles to combine.

## Nutritional Fact per Serving:

Calories: 857; Fat: 36.3g; Total Carbs: 12.4g; Fiber: 2.4g; Net Carbs: 10g; Protein: 26.1g

# MAIN MEALS

## Meatless Florentine Pizza

Pizzas are often hard to have on a keto diet, so making them with flours that are keto safe sets you up on a pizza spree with no limits. This is what you get in this mushroom enriched pizza.

**PREPARATION TIME: 10 MINUTES • COOKING TIME: 25 MINUTES • SERVES: 2**

## Ingredients:

*For the pizza crust:*

6 eggs
1 cup shredded provolone cheese
1 tsp Italian seasoning

*For the topping:*

2/3 cup tomato sauce
2 cups chopped kale, wilted
½ cup grated mozzarella cheese
1 (7 oz) can sliced mushrooms, drained
4 eggs
Olive oil for drizzling

## Directions:

*For the pizza crust:*

Preheat the oven to 400 F and line a pizza-baking pan with parchment paper.

Crack the eggs into a medium bowl; whisk in the provolone cheese, and Italian seasoning. Spread the mixture on a pizza-baking pan, bake in the oven for 15 minutes or until golden. Remove from the oven and allow cooling for 2 minutes.

*For the pizza:*

Increase the oven's temperature to 450 F.

Spread the tomato sauce on the crust, top with the kale, mozzarella, and mushrooms. Bake in the oven for 8 minutes.

Crack the eggs on top and continue baking until the eggs are set, 2 to 3 minutes.

## Nutritional Fact per Serving:

Calories: 646; Fat: 39.1g; Total Carbs: 8.4g; Fiber: 3.5g; Net Carbs: 4.9g; Protein: 36.8g

# Cheesy Mushroom Pie

When making mushrooms pie on the keto diet, the best option to extract your macros is to load it up with cream and cheese. You will have both fat and vitamin essentials guaranteed.

**PREPARATION TIME: 12 MINUTES • COOKING TIME: 43 MINUTES • SERVES: 4**

## Ingredients:

*For the piecrust:*

¼ cup almond flour + extra for dusting
3 tbsp coconut flour
½ tsp salt
¼ cup butter, cold and crumbled

3 tbsp erythritol
1 ½ tsp vanilla extract
4 whole eggs

*For the filling:*

2 tbsp butter
1 medium yellow onion
2 garlic cloves, minced
2 cups mixed mushrooms, chopped
1 green bell pepper, deseeded and diced
1 cup green beans, cut into 3 pieces each
Salt and black pepper to taste

¼ cup heavy cream
1/3 cup sour cream
½ cup almond milk
2 eggs, lightly beaten
¼ tsp nutmeg powder
1 tbsp chopped parsley
1 cup grated Monterey Jack cheese

## Directions:

*For the pastry crust:*

Preheat the oven to 350 F and grease a pie pan with cooking spray

In a large bowl, mix the almond flour, coconut flour, and salt.

Add the butter and mix with an electric hand mixer until crumbly. Add the erythritol and vanilla extract until mixed in. Then, pour in the eggs one after another while mixing until formed into a ball.

Flatten the dough a clean flat surface, cover in plastic wrap, and refrigerate for 1 hour.

After, lightly dust a clean flat surface with almond flour, unwrap the dough, and roll out the dough into a large rectangle, ½ - inch thickness and fit into a pie pan.

Pour some baking beans onto the pastry and bake in the oven until golden. Remove after, pour the beans, and allow cooling.

*For the filling:*

Melt the butter in a skillet and sauté the onion and garlic until softened and fragrant, 3 minutes. Add the mushrooms, bell pepper, green beans, salt and black pepper; cook for 5 minutes.

In a medium bowl, beat the heavy cream, sour cream, milk, and eggs. Season with black pepper, salt, and nutmeg. Stir in the parsley and cheese.

Spread the mushroom mixture in the baked pastry and spread the cheese filling on top. Place the pie in the oven and bake for 30 to 35 minutes or until a toothpick inserted into the pie comes out clean and golden on top.

Remove, let cool for 10 minutes, slice, and serve with roasted tomato salad.

### Nutritional Fact per Serving:

Calories: 527; Fat: 43.6g; Total Carbs: 8.7g; Fiber: 2.2g; Net Carbs: 6.5g; Protein: 21.3g

# Pesto Tofu Zoodles

*I got tired of zoodles with tofu balls sauce, so I tested the dish with some pesto. If it didn't taste terrific, I wouldn't have added it here. You need no further proof than to try it as soon as possible.*

**PREPARATION TIME: 5 MINUTES • COOKING TIME: 12 MINUTES • SERVES: 4**

### Ingredients:

2 tbsp olive oil
1 medium white onion, chopped
1 garlic clove, minced
2 (14 oz) blocks firm tofu, pressed and cubed
1 medium red bell pepper, deseeded and sliced
6 medium zucchinis, spiralized

Salt and black pepper to taste
¼ cup basil pesto, olive oil based
2/3 cup grated Pecorino Romano cheese
½ cup shredded mozzarella cheese
Toasted pine nuts to garnish

### Directions:

Heat the olive oil in a medium pot over medium heat; sauté the onion and garlic until softened and fragrant, 3 minutes.

Add the tofu and cook until golden on all sides then pour in the bell pepper and cook until softened, 4 minutes.

Mix in the zucchinis, pour the pesto on top, and season with salt and black pepper. Cook for 3 to 4 minutes or until the zucchinis soften a little bit. Turn the heat off and carefully stir in the pecorino cheese.

Dish into four plates, share the mozzarella cheese on top, garnish with the pine nuts, and serve warm.

### Nutritional Fact per Serving:

Calories: 477; Fat: 32g; Total Carbs: 12; Fiber: 6.6g; Net Carbs: 5.4g; Protein: 20.4

# Spinach, Kale & Mushroom Biryani

Biryanis rock always – at the Indian restaurant or when made at home. But, did you know that you could bake this cauliflower rice dish? I learned a few tricks online, applied them with my twist of ingredients and it passed for excellence! Here's my version for you.

**PREPARATION TIME: 15 MINUTES • COOKING TIME: 1 HOUR 5 MINUTES • SERVES: 4**

## Ingredients:

6 cups cauli rice
2 tbsp water
Salt and black pepper
3 tbsp ghee
3 medium white onions, chopped
6 garlic cloves, minced
1 tsp ginger puree
1 tbsp turmeric powder + more for dusting
2 cups chopped tomatoes
1 habanero pepper, minced

1 tbsp tomato puree
1 cup sliced cremini mushrooms
1 cup diced paneer cheese
½ cup spinach, chopped
½ cup kale, chopped
1/3 cup water
¼ cup chopped parsley
1 cup Greek yogurt
Olive oil for drizzling

## Directions:

Preheat the oven to 400 F.

Pour the cauli rice into a safe microwave bowl, drizzle with the water, cover with plastic wrap, and microwave for 1 minute or until softened. Remove and season with salt and black pepper. Set aside.

Melt the ghee in a large shallow safe oven pan and sauté the onion, garlic, ginger puree, and turmeric powder. Cook for 15 minutes or until golden, stirring regularly.

Add the tomatoes, habanero, and tomato puree; cook for 5 minutes or until the tomatoes soften.

Stir in the mushrooms, paneer cheese, spinach, kale, and water; season with salt and black pepper and simmer for 15 minutes or until the mushrooms soften. Turn the heat off and stir in the yogurt.

Spoon half of the stew into a bowl and set aside. Sprinkle half of the parsley on the stew in the pan, half of the cauli rice, and dust with the turmeric. Repeat the layering process a second time with the remaining ingredients including the reserved stew.

Drizzle with olive oil and bake in the oven for 25 minutes or until golden and crisp on top.

Remove; allow cooling, and serve almond flour poppadum and coconut chutney.

## Nutritional Fact per Serving:

Calories: 346; Fat: 21.4g; Total Carbs: 8.6g; Fiber: 6.6g; Net Carbs: 2g; Protein: 16g

# Margherita Pizza with Broccoli Crust

For this margarita pizza, swap the meat option for vegan ham and top with some cottage cheese or ricotta cheese, and basil. It turns out yummy.

**PREPARATION TIME: 8 MINUTES • COOKING TIME: 30 MINUTES • SERVES: 2**

## Ingredients:

*For the pizza crust:*

1 small head broccoli, riced
4 eggs
¼ cup shredded cheddar cheese

¼ cup Parmesan cheese
Salt and black pepper to taste
½ tsp Italian seasoning mix

*For the topping:*

6 tbsp tomato sauce
2 ½ oz cremini mushrooms, sliced
1 small red onion, thinly sliced

½ cup cottage cheese
½ tbsp. olive oil
A handful fresh basil

## Directions:

*For the pizza crust:*

Preheat the oven 400 F and line a baking sheet with parchment paper.

Pour the broccoli in a safe microwave bowl, cover with plastic wrap and microwave for 1 to 2 minutes or until softened. Remove after and allow cooling.

Squeeze the riced broccoli in cheesecloth until as much liquid has been extracted and transfer to a mixing bowl.

Crack in the eggs, add the cheeses, salt, black pepper, and Italian seasoning; whisk until evenly combined. Spread the mixture on the baking sheet and bake in the oven for 15 minutes or until the golden. Remove from the oven and allow cooling for 2 minutes.

*For the pizza:*

Spread the tomato sauce on the crust, scatter with the mushrooms, onion, and the cottage cheese; drizzle with the olive oil. Place the pan in the oven and bake for 15 minutes or until golden.

Remove after, scatter with the basil leaves, slice, and serve.

## Nutritional Fact per Serving:

Calories: 290; Fat: 22.5g; Total Carbs: 6.6g; Fiber: 5.8g; Net Carbs: 0.8g; Protein: 12.8g

# Tofu Loaf with Walnuts

The festive seasons should be here soon. Make this tofu loaf for your vegetarian and non-vegetarian guests alike. It is sumptuous in all its senses and makes for a family bonding delicacy.

**PREPARATION TIME: 10 MINUTES • COOKING TIME: 1 HOUR • SERVES: 4**

## Ingredients:

3 tbsp olive oil + extra for brushing
2 white onions, finely chopped
4 garlic cloves, minced
1 lb firm tofu, pressed and cubed
2 tbsp soy sauce
¾ cup chopped walnuts
Salt and black pepper

1 tbsp dried Italian mixed herbs
½ tsp swerve sugar
¼ cup golden flaxseed meal
1 tbsp sesame seeds
1 green bell pepper, deseeded and chopped
1 medium red bell pepper, deseeded and chopped
½ cup tomato sauce

## Directions:

Preheat an oven to 350 F and lightly brush an 8 x 4 inch loaf pan with olive oil. Set aside.

In a bowl, combine the olive oil, onion, garlic, tofu, soy sauce, walnuts, salt, black pepper, Italian mixed herbs, swerve sugar, golden flaxseed meal and mix with your hands.

Pour the mixture into a bowl and stir in the sesame seeds and the green and red bell peppers.

Transfer the tofu loaf into the pan and mold to fit into the container; spoon the tomato sauce on top. Bake in the oven for 45 minutes to 1 hour. Turn the food onto a chopping board, slice, and serve with oregano-sautéed cauliflower and steamed green beans.

## Nutritional Fact per Serving:

Calories: 432; Fat: 31.4g; Total Carbs: 8.7g; Fiber: 6.2g; Net Carbs: 2.5g; Protein: 24.3g

# Roasted Soy Chorizo and Mixed Greens

Want to bake some vegetables, but need some fatty elements? Work with some soy chorizo, olive oil, and your essentials will be met.

**PREPARATION TIME: 15 MINUTES • COOKING TIME: 15 MINUTES • SERVES: 4**

## Ingredients:

1 lb soy chorizo, cubed
1 lb asparagus, trimmed and halved
2 green and red bell peppers, deseeded and diced
1 cup green beans, trimmed
2 red onions, cut into wedges

1 head medium broccoli, cut into florets
Salt and black pepper to taste
4 tbsp olive oil
1 tbsp maple (sugar-free) syrup
1 lemon, juiced

## Directions:

Preheat the oven to 400 F.

On a baking tray, add the soy chorizo, asparagus, bell peppers, green beans, onions, and broccoli; season with salt, black pepper, and drizzle with olive oil and maple syrup. Use your hands to rub the seasoning onto the vegetables.

Place in the oven and bake for 15 minutes or until the vegetables soften and become golden at the edges. Remove from the oven, drizzle with lemon juice, and serve warm.

## Nutritional Fact per Serving:

Calories: 300; Fat: 18.5g; Total Carbs: 12.5g; Fiber: 9.2g; Net Carbs: 3.3g; Protein: 14.8g

# Hazelnuts and Cheese Stuffed Zucchinis

On a keto diet, stuffed zucchinis should never miss your meal plan. Rather, explore the filling with different cheeses, nuts, and sauces. Try this and tell me what you think.

**PREPARATION TIME: 15 MINUTES • COOKING TIME: 20 MINUTES • SERVES: 4**

## Ingredients:

2 tbsp olive oil
1 cup cauliflower rice
¼ cup vegetable broth
1 ¼ cup diced tomatoes
1 medium red onion, chopped
¼ cup pine nuts

¼ cup hazelnuts
4 tbsp chopped cilantro
1 tbsp balsamic vinegar
1 tbsp smoked paprika
4 medium zucchinis, halved
1 cup grated Monterey Jack cheese

## Directions:

Preheat the oven to 350 F.

Pour the cauli rice and vegetable broth in a medium pot and cook over medium heat for 5 minutes or until softened. Turn the heat off, fluff the cauli rice, and allow cooling.

Scoop the flesh out of the zucchini halves using a spoon and chop the pulp. Brush the inner parts of the vegetable with olive oil.

In a bowl, mix the cauliflower rice, tomatoes, red onion, pine nuts, hazelnuts, cilantro, balsamic vinegar, paprika, zucchini pulp, salt, and pepper. Spoon the mixture into the zucchini halves, drizzle with more olive oil, and sprinkle the cheese on top.

Place the stuffed vegetables on a baking sheet and bake in the oven for 15 to 20 minutes or until the cheese has melted and golden. Remove, allow cooling, and serve.

## Nutritional Fact per Serving:

Calories: 330; Fat: 28g; Total Carbs: 10.6g; Fiber: 5.4g; Net Carbs: 5.2g; Protein: 12.3g

# Mushroom Pizza Bowls with Avocado & Cilantro

I love this pizza bowls For the avocado, mushroom, and chili blend. When looking for a way to make a pizza quickly, these bowls are your best tries.

**PREPARATION TIME: 20 MINUTES • COOKING TIME: 20 MINUTES • SERVES: 4**

## Ingredients:

1 ½ cups cauli rice
2 tbsp water
Olive oil for brushing
2 cups pizza sauce
1 cup grated Monterey Jack Cheese
1 cup grated mozzarella cheese
½ cup sliced white mushrooms
2 large tomatoes, chopped
1 small red onion, chopped
1 tsp dried oregano
2 jalapeño peppers, deseeded and chopped
Salt and black pepper to taste
1 avocado, halved, pitted, and chopped
¼ cup chopped cilantro

## Directions:

Preheat the oven to 400 F.

Pour the cauli rice into a safe microwave bowl, drizzle with 2 tablespoons of water, and steam in the microwave for 1 to 2 minutes. Remove, fluff with a fork, and set aside.

Lightly brush the inner parts of four medium ramekins with the olive oil and spread half of the pizza sauce at the bottom of each. Top with half of the cauli rice and half of the cheeses.

In a bowl, mix the mushrooms, tomatoes, onions, oregano, jalapeño peppers, salt, and black pepper. Spoon half of the mixture into the ramekin and repeat the layering process with the remaining ingredients finishing off with the cheese.

Bake in the oven for 20 minutes or until the cheese melts and is golden on top.

Remove and top with the avocados and cilantro; allow cooling for 5 minutes, and serve with arugula and olive salad.

## Nutritional Fact per Serving:

Calories: 378; Fat: 22.5g; Total Carbs: 12.3g; Fiber: 8.9g; Net Carbs: 3.4g; Protein: 20.6g

# Tempeh Taco Cups

These mini taco cups are cute to serve the little when trying to avoid the excess carbs and sugars. It sits in the right filling that kids love; that tanginess though.

**PREPARATION TIME: 10 MINUTES • COOKING TIME: 21 MINUTES • SERVES: 4**

## Ingredients:

4 low carb tortilla wraps
2 tsp melted butter
1 tbsp olive oil
1 small yellow onion, finely chopped
½ cup tempeh, crumbled
1 tsp smoked paprika
½ tsp cumin powder
Salt and black pepper to taste
1 small iceberg lettuce, 8 firm leaves extracted
1 medium red bell pepper, deseeded and chopped
1 ripe avocado, halved and pitted
1 small lemon, juiced
¼ cup sour cream

## Directions:

Preheat the oven to 400 F.

Divide each tortilla wrap into two, lay on a chopping board, and brush with butter. Line 8 muffin tins with the tortilla and bake in the oven for 8 to 9 minutes or until the edges crisp and lightly golden. Remove from the oven and set aside to cool.

Heat the olive oil in a skillet and sauté the onion for 3 minutes. Crumble the tempeh into the pan and cook for 8 minutes or until deep brown. Stir in the paprika, cumin, salt, black pepper and cook for 1 minute.

To assemble, fit the lettuce leaves into the tortilla cups, share the tempeh mixture on top, top with the bell pepper, avocado, and drizzle with the lemon juice. Add the sour cream and serve immediately.

## Nutritional Fact per Serving:

Calories: 220; Fat: 17g; Total Carbs: 9.3g; Fiber: 5.5g; Net Carbs: 3.8g; Protein: 6.7g

# Tofu Meatballs with Creamy Cauli Mash

For obese kids, the ketogenic diet is an excellent recommendation. And because kids love meatballs with pasta, swapping meat with tofu and pasta with zoodles creates delicious, nutritious options For the kids.

**PREPARATION TIME: 15 MINUTES • COOKING TIME: 47 MINUTES • SERVES: 4**

## Ingredients:

*For the tofu balls and sauce:*

1 lb silken tofu, pressed and cubed
2 garlic cloves, minced
2 small red onions, chopped
1 cup white button mushrooms, chopped
1 tsp dried basil
Salt and black pepper to taste

1 small red bell pepper, deseeded and chopped
½ cup golden flaxseed meal
½ almond milk
1 ½ + 1 tbsp. olive oil
2 cups tomato sauce
4 to 6 fresh basil leaves to garnish

*For the cauliflower mash:*

1 lb cauliflower, cut into florets
1 cup water, for steaming
Salt and black pepper to taste

2 tbsp butter
½ cup heavy cream
¼ cup grated Parmesan cheese

## Directions:

*For the tofu balls and sauce:*

Preheat the oven to 350 F and line a baking tray with parchment paper.

In a bowl, add the silken tofu, half of the garlic, half of the onion, mushrooms, basil, salt, and black pepper; mix with your hands until evenly combined. Pour the mixture into a bowl and mold bite-size balls out of the mixture.

Place the flaxseed meal and almond milk each in a shallow dish.

Dip each ball in the almond milk and then in the flaxseed meal. Place on the baking sheet and bake in the oven for 10 minutes or until properly compacted.

Heat 1 ½ tbsp of olive oil in a medium pot, remove the tofu balls from the oven, and fry in the oil until golden brown on all sides. Remove onto a paper towel-lined plate and set aside.

Heat the remaining oil in a saucepan and sauté the onion, garlic, and bell pepper into the oil and sauté until fragrant and soft. Pour in the tomato sauce and cook 20 minutes or until s stew forms. Add the tofu balls, spoon some sauce to cover, and simmer for 5 to 7 minutes.

*For the cauliflower mash:*

In a medium pot, add the cauliflower, water, and a little salt. Bring to a boil for 10 minutes or until the vegetable softens. Drain through a colander and pour into a medium bowl.

Add the butter, salt, and black pepper; mash into a puree using a potato mash.

Stir in the heavy cream and Parmesan cheese until evenly combined.

Spoon the cauli mash into serving bowls, top with some tofu balls and sauce, and garnish with the basil leaves. Serve warm.

## Nutritional Fact per Serving:

Calories: 686; Fat: 30.7g; Total Carbs: 8.7g; Fiber: 3.1g; Net Carbs: 5.6g; Protein: 22.3g

# Tofu Nuggets with Cilantro Dip

Tofu nuggets with this flavorful dip is excellent for a kid's snack. Pack a few in their lunch boxes to snack on during their lunch break.

**PREPARATION TIME: 10 MINUTES • COOKING TIME: 15 MINUTES • SERVES: 4**

## Ingredients:

*For the tofu nuggets:*

1 ½ cups olive oil for frying
2 (14 oz) blocks extra firm tofu, pressed and cut into bite-size cubes

1 egg, lightly beaten
1 cup golden flaxseed meal, seasoned

*For the cilantro dip:*

1 ripe avocado, halved, pitted, and frozen
½ tbsp. chopped cilantro
Salt and black pepper

½ tbsp. olive oil
1 lime, ½ juiced and ½ cut into wedges for serving

## Directions:

*For the tofu nuggets:*

Heat the olive oil in a large deep skillet.

Meanwhile, coat the tofu cubes in the egg and then adequately in the flaxseed meal. Fry in the hot oil in batches until golden brown on all sides. Transfer to a paper towel-lined plate.

*For the cilantro dip.*

Place the avocado, cilantro, salt, black pepper, and lime juice in a blender; puree until very smooth.

Spoon the dip into a serving bowl, plate with the tofu nuggets, garnish with the lime wedges, and serve immediately.

## Nutritional Fact per Serving:

Calories: 665; Fat: 54.6g; Total Carbs: 22g; Fiber: 15.8g; Net Carbs: 6.2g; Protein: 32.6g

# Zucchini- Cranberry Cake Squares

Also, a fantastic option for snack. You can make these and store a few in an airtight container. During the holidays, it will be useful to get the kids through the day.

**PREPARATION TIME: 17 MINUTES • COOKING TIME: 15 MINUTES • SERVES: 6**

## Ingredients:

1 ¼ cup chopped zucchinis
2 tbsp olive oil
½ cup dried cranberries
1 lemon, zested
3 eggs

1 ½ cups almond flour
½ tsp baking powder
1 tsp cinnamon powder
A pinch salt

## Directions:

Preheat the oven to 350 F and line a square cake tin with parchment paper.

Pour the zucchinis into a colander, sprinkle with salt, and allow sitting for 5 minutes. After, squeeze out as much liquid from the vegetable and transfer to a large mixing bowl.

Add the olive oil, cranberries, lemon zest, and eggs until evenly combined.

Sift the flour, baking powder, and cinnamon powder into the mixture and fold with the salt.

Pour the mixture into the cake tin and bake in the oven for 30 minutes or until the cake turns golden and a toothpick inserted into the cake comes out clean.

Remove; allow cooling in the tin for 10 minutes and transfer the cake to a wire rack to cool completely. Cut into squares and serve the kids for snack.

## Nutritional Fact per Serving:

Calories: 121; Fat: 10.2g; Total Carbs: 3.6g; Fiber: 1.1g; Net Carbs: 2.5g; Protein: 4.5g

# Strawberry Faux Oats

So, oats are not keto certified but kids love them, what do we do? We create a more nutritious option with seeds. It turns out amazing.

**PREPARATION TIME: 10 MINUTES • COOKING TIME: 10 MINUTES • SERVES: 2**

## Ingredients:

2 tbsp coconut flour
2 tbsp golden flaxseed meal
2 tbsp chia seeds
2 tbsp heavy cream
½ cup almond milk

3 tbsp maple syrup, sugar-free
1 tsp vanilla extract
1 cup frozen strawberries, halved
¼ cup desiccated coconut

## Directions:

Combine the coconut flour, flaxseed meal, and chia seeds in a small saucepan. Stir in the heavy cream, almond milk, maple syrup, and vanilla extract.

Place the pan over medium heat, whisk the ingredients until thick and warmed through, 10 minutes.

Pour the mixture into two serving bowls and top with the strawberries and desiccated coconut. Drizzle with some more maple syrup for more sweetness and serve warm.

## Nutritional Fact per Serving:

Calories: 289; Fat: 18.5g; Total Carbs: 17.4g; Fiber: 11.3g; Net Carbs: 6.1g; Protein: 5.8g

# Cheese Quesadillas with Fruit Salad

Don't serve their quesadillas as they are any further. Pair them with this berry-yogurt to nourish their bodies better and give them something more delicious.

**PREPARATION TIME: 5 MINUTES • COOKING TIME: 2 MINUTES • SERVES: 2**

## Ingredients:

*For the quesadillas:*

2 large low carb tortillas
1 cup grated cheddar cheese

2 small green onions, chopped

*For the fruit salad:*

1 cup mixed berries
½ tsp cinnamon powder
½ lemon, juiced

1 cup Greek yogurt
Maple (sugar-free) syrup to taste

## Directions:

Divide the tortillas into two, top half each with the cheddar cheese and spring onion, and cover with the halves.

Place in a large non- stick skillet and heat until golden and the cheese melted. Remove onto a plate, allow cooling, and cut into four wedges.

For the salad, combine the berries, cinnamon powder, lemon juice, Greek yogurt, and maple syrup in a bowl. Divide into two bowls and serve with the quesadillas.

## Nutritional Fact per Serving:

Calories: 135; Fat: 13.5g; Total Carbs: 4.8g; Fiber: 1.8g; Net Carbs: 3g; Protein: 3.5g

# Tofu Radish Bowls

When in a hurry to make breakfast, throwing these essential ingredients creates a sumptuous, easy dish For the children. It gets ready quickly and turns out tasty.

**PREPARATION TIME: 15 MINUTES • COOKING TIME: 20 MINUTES • SERVES: 4**

## Ingredients:

1 tbsp + 1 tbsp olive oil
1 (14 oz) block extra firm tofu, pressed and cubed
1 ½ cup shredded radishes
½ cup chopped white onions
2 yellow bell peppers, deseeded and chopped
Salt and black pepper to taste

¼ cup chopped baby bella mushrooms
4 eggs
1/3 cup tomato salsa
A handful chopped parsley
1 ripe avocado, pitted and chopped

## Directions:

Heat 1 tablespoon of olive oil in a skillet over medium heat and add the tofu, radishes, onions, and bell peppers. Season with salt and black pepper; cook for 4 minutes on each side or until the tofu is slightly golden.

Pour in the mushrooms, continue cooking until the vegetable crisp and turn golden brown. Divide into four bowls.

Heat the remaining olive oil in the skillet, crack an egg each into the pan, and cook until the white sets, but the yolk quite runny.

Transfer to the top of one tofu-radish hash bowl and make the remaining eggs. Top the bowls with the tomato salsa, parsley, and avocado. Serve immediately.

## Nutritional Fact per Serving:

Calories: 353; Fat: 25g; Total Carbs: 17.2g; Fiber: 11.3g; Net Carbs: 5.9g; Protein: 19.9g

# Cauliflower and Halloumi Packets

Food parcels are romantic food options, but these mini ones for older children a creative way of teaching the kids how to cook. Make these parcels with them and watch them have fun filling up the packets.

**PREPARATION TIME: 10 MINUTES • COOKING TIME: 15 MINUTES • SERVES: 4**

## Ingredients:

2 heads cauliflower, chopped roughly
¼ cup vegetable broth
1 lemon, juiced
2 tbsp maple (sugar-free) syrup

1 red bell pepper, deseeded and chopped
1 orange bell pepper, deseeded and chopped
¼ cup cubed halloumi
Olive oil to drizzle

## Directions:

Place a baking tray in the oven and preheat the oven to 350 F.

Place the cauliflower in a food processor and pulse a few times until a coarse consistency is achieved but not riced to make the couscous. Pour the couscous and vegetable stock into a medium pot; cook over medium heat until slightly softened, 2 to 3 minutes. Drain afterwards using a sieve and set aside.

In a small bowl, whisk the lemon juice and maple syrup, and set aside. Cut out two 2 x 15 inches parchment papers onto a flat surface spoon the couscous in the middle of each, top with the bell peppers, halloumi, and drizzle the dressing on top. Wrap the papers into parcels and place on the baking tray; cook for 10 to 15 minutes. When ready, remove and carefully open the pouches to allow the steam escape. Serve warm.

## Nutritional Fact per Serving:

Calories: 240; Fat: 19g; Total Carbs: 6.9g; Fiber: 4.2g; Net Carbs: 4.7g; Protein: 5.1g

# Egg Cauli Fried Rice with Grilled Cheese

Fried rice is one of the kids' favorites. But since we can't have fried or grilled chicken with these, grilling some halloumi and loading the cauli rice with eggs, does the perfect trick.

**PREPARATION TIME: 5 MINUTES • COOKING TIME: 5 MINUTES • SERVES: 4**

## Ingredients:

1 tbsp ghee
4 eggs, beaten
1 green bell pepper, deseeded and chopped
¼ cup green beans, trimmed and chopped
2 cups cauliflower rice, steamed

1 tsp soy sauce
Salt and black pepper to taste
2 tbsp chopped parsley
½ lb halloumi, cut into ¼ to ½ inch slabs

## Directions:

Melt the ghee in a skillet over medium heat and pour in the eggs. Swirl the pan to spread the eggs around and start splitting with a ladle once beginning to set; cook for 1 minute.

Move the scrambled eggs to the side of the skillet, add bell pepper and green beans, and sauté for 3 minutes. Pour in the cauli rice and cook for 2 minutes. Top with soy sauce, salt, and pepper; combine evenly, and cook for 2 minutes. Dish into plates, garnish with the parsley, and set aside.

Preheat a grill pan over medium heat and grill the halloumi on both sides until the cheese lightly browns. Place on the side of the rice and serve warm.

## Nutritional Fact per Serving:

Calories: 275; Fat: 19.5g; Total Carbs: 9.9g; Fiber: 5.4g; Net Carbs: 4.5g; Protein: 15.9g

# Cheesy Broccoli Nachos with Salsa

Nachos are everyone's favorite even little children. I like how broccoli turns out perfectly as nachos, which serves with different types of salsa.

**PREPARATION TIME: 10 MINUTES • COOKING TIME: 20 MINUTES • SERVES: 4**

## Ingredients:

*For the cheesy broccoli nachos:*

2 heads medium broccoli, trimmed and chopped
3 tbsp coconut flour
1 tsp smoked paprika
½ tsp coriander powder

1 tsp cumin powder
½ tsp garlic powder
2 eggs, beaten
¼ cup grated Monterey jack cheese

*For the salsa:*

4 plum tomatoes, finely chopped
½ lime, juiced

4 sprigs cilantro, chopped
1 avocado, halved, pitted, and chopped

## Directions:

Preheat the oven to 350 F.

Pour the broccoli into a food processor and blend into a rice-like consistency. Heat a large skillet over low heat, pour in the broccoli, and dry-fry for 10 minutes or until most of the moisture has evaporated. Transfer to a mixing bowl to cool.

Line two baking sheets with parchment papers and set aside.

Onto the broccoli, add the coconut flour, smoked paprika, coriander powder, cumin powder, garlic powder, and eggs. Mix and use your hands to form into a ball.

Divide into halves, place each half on each baking sheet, and press down into a rough circle. Bake in the oven for 5 to 10 minutes or until golden on both sides.

Take out of the oven, cut into triangles immediately, and sprinkle with the cheese. Allow cooling while you make the salsa.

In a bowl, combine the tomatoes, lime, cilantro, and avocado.

Serve the nachos with the salsa.

## Nutritional Fact per Serving:

Calories: 208; Fat: 12.4g; Total Carbs: 10g; Fiber: 5.5g; Net Carbs: 4.5g; Protein: 7.6g

# DESERTS

## Pistachio Heart Biscuits

Love in the air or just being creative? Maybe being creative is the drill because I play with shapes, dark chocolate, white chocolate, and pistachios to create these lovelies.

**PREPARATION TIME: 10 MINUTES • COOKING TIME: 20 MINUTES + CHILLING TIME • SERVES: 4**

### Ingredients:

1 cup unsalted butter, softened
2/3 cup swerve sugar
1 large egg, beaten
2 tsp pistachio extract

2 cups almond flour + extra for dusting
½ cup unsweetened dark chocolate
Chopped pistachios, to garnish

### Directions:

Add the butter and swerve sugar to a bowl; beat with an electric whisk until smooth and creamy. Whisk in the egg until adequately combined.

Mix in the pistachio extract and almond flour until a smooth dough forms. Wrap the dough in plastic wrap and chill for 10 minutes.

Preheat the oven to 350 F and lightly dust a chopping board with some almond flour. Unwrap the dough and roll out on the chopping board to 2-inch thickness.

Using a heart-shaped cookie cutter, cut out as many biscuits as you can get while rerolling the trimming and making more biscuits.

Arrange the biscuits on the parchment paper-lined baking sheet and bake for 12 to 15 minutes or until crisp at the edges and pale golden.

Remove and transfer to a wire rack to cool completely when ready.

In two separate bowls, melt the chocolate in a microwave while adding some maple syrup for taste.

Dip one side of each biscuit in the dark chocolate and then in the white chocolate. Garnish the dark chocolate's side with the pistachios and allow cooling on the wire rack.

Serve after dinner.

### Nutritional Fact per Serving:

Calories: 470; Fat: 44.5g; Total Carbs: 6.7g; Fiber: 3.2g; Net Carbs: 3.4g; Protein: 6.2g

# Key Lime Truffles

A touch of key lime sets a completely new difference to regular truffles. The tang is right and so is the cocoa flavor.

**PREPARATION TIME: 5 MINUTES + CHILLING TIME • SERVES: 6**

## Ingredients:

2/3 cup heavy cream
2/3 cup unsweetened dark chocolate, roughly chopped

2 tsp lime extract
¼ cup unsweetened cocoa powder mixed with 2 tbsp swerve sugar

## Directions:

Heat the heavy cream in a small pan over low heat until tiny bubbles form around the edges of the pan. Turn the heat off.

Pour the dark chocolate into the pan, swirl the pan to allow the hot cream to spread over the chocolate, and then gently stir the mixture until smooth. Mix in the lime extract and transfer the mixture to a bowl. Refrigerate for 4 hours and more.

Line two baking trays with parchment papers; set one aside and pour the cocoa powder mixture onto the other.

Take out the chocolate mixture; form bite-size balls out of the mix and roll all round in the cocoa powder to completely coat.

Place the truffles on the set aside baking tray and chill in the fridge for 30 minutes before serving.

## Nutritional Fact per Serving:

Calories: 143; Fat: 12.6g; Total Carbs: 3.1g; Fiber: 2.5g; Net Carbs: 0.6g; Protein: 2.4g

# Raspberry and Red Wine Crumble

Crumbles never leave my dessert options because they are simple to make and yet delicious. Adding red wine changes things up here for me, which brings on a worth of flavor that is irresistible.

**PREPARATION TIME: 10 MINUTES • COOKING TIME: 45 MINUTES • SERVES: 6**

## Ingredients:

2 cups raspberries
¼ cup red wine
1 teaspoon cinnamon
1 ¼ cup erythritol, divided
1 tsp vanilla extract

1 cup salted butter, cubed
1 ½ cups almond flour
¾ cup coconut flour

## Directions:

Preheat the oven 375 F.

In a baking dish, add the raspberries, red wine, half of the erythritol, vanilla extract, and stir.

In a bowl, rub the butter with the almond flour, coconut flour, and erythritol until resembles large breadcrumbs.

Spoon the mixture to cover the raspberries, place in the oven, and bake for 45 minutes or until the top looks golden brown. Remove; cool for 3 minutes, and serve warm.

## Nutritional Fact per Serving:

Calories: 318; Fat: 31.3g; Total Carbs: 9.7g; Fiber: 4.9g; Net Carbs: 4.8g; Protein: 1.5g

# Dark Chocolate Cake

Each bite will melt in your mouth with subtle tastes that are perfect for pushing down a heavy meal. Enjoy the decadence!

**PREPARATION TIME: 10 MINUTES • COOKING TIME: 45 MINUTES • SERVES: 4**

## Ingredients:

½ cup olive oil
1 cup almond flour
½ cup unsweetened dark chocolate, melted
1 cup swerve sugar
2 tsp vanilla bean paste

½ tsp salt
2 tsp cinnamon powder
½ cup boiling water
3 large eggs

## Directions:

Preheat the oven to 350 F and lightly grease a springform pan with cooking spray and line with parchment paper.

In a large bowl, evenly combine the olive oil, almond flour, chocolate, swerve sugar, vanilla bean paste, salt, cinnamon powder, and boiling water. Crack the eggs one after the other while beating until smooth.

Pour the batter into the springform pan and bake in the oven for 45 minutes or until a toothpick inserted comes out clean.

Take out from the oven; allow cooling in the pan for 10 minutes, then turn over onto a wire rack.

Dust with swerve confectioner's sugar slice, and serve.

## Nutritional Fact per Serving:

Calories: 417; Fat: 41.7g; Total Carbs: 11.5g; Fiber: 9.8g; Net Carbs: 1.7g; Protein: 16.4g

# Mint Chocolate Cheesecake

The next time you make a cheesecake, add some white chocolate and mint extract. Try it and remember to save me some slices.

**PREPARATION TIME: 10 MINUTES • COOKING TIME: 5 MINUTES + CHILLING TIME • SERVES: 4**

## Ingredients:

*For the crust:*

1 cup raw almonds
½ cup salted butter, melted

2 tbsp swerve sugar

*For the cake:*

4 tbsp unsalted butter, melted
2 gelatin sheets
2 tbsp lime juice
2/3 cup unsweetened dark chocolate, chopped

1 ½ cups cream cheese
½ cup swerve sugar
1 cup Greek yogurt
1 tbsp mint extract

## Directions:

*For the crust:*

Preheat the oven to 350 F.

In a blender, process the almonds until finely ground. Add the butter and sweetener, and mix until combined. Press the crust mixture into the bottom of the cake pan until firm. Bake for 5 minutes. Place in the fridge to chill afterward.

*For the cake:*

In a small pot, combine the gelatin with the lime juice, and a tablespoon of water. Allow sitting for 5 minutes and then, place the pot over medium heat to dissolve the gelatin. Set aside.

Pour the dark chocolate in a bowl and melt in the microwave for 1 minute, stirring at every 10 seconds interval. Set aside.

In another, beat the cream cheese and swerve sugar using an electric mixer until smooth. Stir in the yogurt and gelatin until evenly combined. After, fold in the melted dark chocolate and then the mint extract.

Remove the pan from the fridge and pour the cream mixture on top. Tap the side gently to release any trapped air bubbles and transfer to the fridge to chip for 3 hours or more.

Remove and release the pan's locker, garnish the top with more dark chocolate, and slice.

## Nutritional Fact per Serving:

Calories: 235g; Fat: 14.1g; Total Carbs: 7.3g; Fiber: 3.5g; Net Carbs: 3.8g; Protein: 6.7g

# Red Berries Fat Bombs

The assembling process of these fat bombs is worth every bit of your effort. The result is a mouthful of fresh red berries with hints of cheese.

**PREPARATION TIME: 15 MINUTES • COOKING TIME: 5 MINUTES + CHILLING TIME • SERVES: 4**

## Ingredients:

1 cup strawberries
1 cup raspberries + extra to garnish
1 cup cranberries
1 tsp vanilla extract

16 oz cream cheese, room temperature
4 tbsp unsalted butter
2 tbsp maple (sugar-free) syrup

## Directions:

Line a muffin tray with liners and set aside. Puree the fruits in a blender with the vanilla. In a small saucepan, melt the cream cheese and butter together over medium heat until mixed.

Then, in a medium bowl, combine the fruit, cheese mixtures, and maple syrup evenly and fill the muffin tray with the mix. Refrigerate for 40 minutes and serve after.

## Nutritional Fact per Serving:

Calories: 227g; Fat: 14.8g; Total Carbs: 5.2g; Fiber: 2.1g; Net Carbs: 3.1g; Protein: 4.6g

# Blueberry Smoothie

Smoothies are one of my favorite ways to wash down a hearty dinner and so I make sure to load this one with some creamy goodness. Sip with love!

**PREPARATION TIME: 5 MINUTES • SERVES: 4**

## Ingredients:

2 cups fresh blueberries
1 cup almond milk
½ cup heavy cream
Maple (sugar-free) syrup to taste

2 tbsp sesame seeds
Chopped pistachios for topping
1 tbsp chopped mint leaves

## Directions:

Combine the blueberries, milk, heavy cream, and syrup in a blender. Process until smooth and pour into serving glasses. Top with the sesame seeds, pistachios, and mint leaves.

## Nutritional Fact per Serving:

Calories: 228g; Fat: 19.6g; Total Carbs: 4.8g; Fiber: 3.7g; Net Carbs: 1g; Protein: 5.8g

# Speedy Custard Tart

Adding some fruits to these will have made some extra difference, but when not able to have these fruits on the keto diet, you work out the goodness in the custard. The result of this is a blessing.

**PREPARATION TIME: 15 MINUTES • COOKING TIME: 1 HOUR • SERVES: 4**

## Ingredients:

### For the piecrust:

¼ cup almond flour + extra for dusting
3 tbsp coconut flour
½ tsp salt
¼ cup butter, cold and crumbled

3 tbsp erythritol
1 ½ tsp vanilla extract
4 whole eggs

### For the filling:

2 whole eggs + 3 egg yolks
½ cup swerve sugar
1 tsp vanilla bean paste
2 tbsp coconut flour

1 ¼ cup almond milk
1 ¼ cup heavy cream
1 ½ tbsp. maple (sugar-free) syrup
¼ cup chopped almonds

## Directions:

### For the piecrust:

Preheat the oven to 350 F and grease a pie pan with cooking spray

In a large bowl, mix the almond flour, coconut flour, and salt.

Add the butter and mix with an electric hand mixer until crumbly. Add the erythritol and vanilla extract until mixed in. Then, pour in the four eggs one after another while mixing until formed into a ball.

After, lightly dust a clean flat surface with almond flour, unwrap the dough, and roll out the dough into a large rectangle, ½ - inch thickness and fit into a pie pan.

Pour some baking beans onto the pastry and bake in the oven until golden. Remove after, pour the beans, and allow cooling.

### For the filling:

In a large mixing bowl, whisk the 2 whole eggs, 3 egg yolks, swerve sugar, vanilla bean paste, and coconut flour.

Put the almond milk, heavy cream, and maple syrup into a medium pot and bring to a boil over medium heat. Pour the mixture into the egg mix and whisk while pouring.

Run the batter through a fine strainer into a bowl and skim off any froth.

Take out the pie pastry from the oven, pour out the baking beans, remove the parchment paper, and transfer the egg batter into the pie. Bake in the oven for 40 to 50 minutes or until the custard sets with a slight wobble in the center.

1Garnish with the chopped almonds, slice, and serve when slightly cooled.

## Nutritional Fact per Serving:

Calories: 459; Fat: 40.7g; Total Carbs: 6.8g; Fiber: 5.6g; Net Carbs: 1.2g; Protein: 11.5g

# Zucchini Cake Slices

Zucchini in everything just works, which is amazing. For carrot cake swap, use grated zucchinis to fill the batter and watch it bake to perfection.

**PREPARATION TIME: 10 MINUTES • COOKING TIME: 20 MINUTES + 2 HOUR REFRIGERATION • SERVES: 4**

## Ingredients:

1 cup butter, softened + extra for greasing
1 cup erythritol
4 eggs
2/3 cup coconut flour
2 tsp baking powder

2/3 cup ground almonds
1 lemon, zested and juiced
1 cup finely grated zucchini
1 cup crème fraiche, for serving
1 tbsp chopped walnuts

## Directions:

Preheat the oven to 375 F, grease a springform pan with cooking spray, and line with parchment paper.

In a bowl, beat the butter and erythritol until creamy and pale. Add the eggs one after another while whisking. Sift the coconut flour and baking powder into the mixture and stir along with the ground almonds, lemon zest, juice, and zucchini.

Spoon the mixture into the springform pan and bake in the oven for 40 minutes or until risen and a toothpick inserted into the cake comes out clean.

Remove the cake from the oven when ready; allow cooling in the pan for 10 minutes, and transfer to a wire rack.

Spread the crème fraiche on top of the cake and sprinkle with the walnuts. Slice and serve.

## Nutritional Fact per Serving:

Calories: 778; Fat: 70.5g; Total Carbs: 4.4g; Fiber: 0.7g; Net Carbs: 3.7g; Protein: 31.9g

# Strawberry Blackberry Pie

Ah huh! Something to rush family lunch for. When this pie comes out, you'll be in awe at the outcome, you may not want to break into it. But, the beauty that you feel on your tongue is unexplainable.

**PREPARATION TIME: 10 MINUTES • COOKING TIME: 20 MINUTES + 2 HOUR REFRIGERATION • SERVES: 4**

## Ingredients:

*For the piecrust:*

¼ cup almond flour + extra for dusting
3 tbsp coconut flour
½ tsp salt
¼ cup butter, cold and crumbled

3 tbsp erythritol
1 ½ tsp vanilla extract
4 whole eggs

*For the filling:*

2 ¼ cup strawberries and blackberries
1 cup erythritol + extra for sprinkling

1 vanilla pod, bean paste extracted
1 egg, beaten

## Directions:

Preheat the oven to 350 F and grease a pie pan with cooking spray

In a large bowl, mix the almond flour, coconut flour, and salt.

Add the butter and mix with an electric hand mixer until crumbly. Add the erythritol and vanilla extract until mixed in. Then, pour in the 4 eggs one after another while mixing until formed into a ball.

Flatten the dough a clean flat surface, cover in plastic wrap, and refrigerate for 1 hour.

After, lightly dust a clean flat surface with almond flour, unwrap the dough, and roll out the dough into a large rectangle, ½ - inch thickness and fit into a pie pan.

Pour some baking beans onto the pastry and bake in the oven until golden. Remove after, pour pout the baking beans, and allow cooling.

In a bowl, mix the berries, erythritol, and vanilla bean paste. Spoon the mixture into the pie, level with a spoon, and use the pastry strips to create a lattice top over the berries. Brush with the beaten egg, sprinkle with more erythritol, and bake for 30 minutes or until the fruit is bubbling and the pie golden brown.

Remove from the oven, allow cooling, slice, and serve with whipped cream.

## Nutritional Fact per Serving:

Calories: 262; Fat: 21.7g; Total Carbs: 4.8g; Fiber: 1.8g; Net Carbs: 3g; Protein: 8.9g

# Blackberry Lemon Tarte Tatin

Making this French classic with blackberries taught me new things about blackberries. The fruits baked very soft and oozed out some good amount of juices, which slightly softened the puff pastry for an easy spoon in. It turned out perfect.

**PREPARATION TIME: 10 MINUTES • COOKING TIME: 40 MINUTES • SERVES: 4**

## Ingredients:

*For the piecrust:*

¼ cup almond flour + extra for dusting
3 tbsp coconut flour
½ tsp salt
¼ cup butter, cold and crumbled

3 tbsp erythritol
1 ½ tsp vanilla extract
4 whole eggs

*For the filling:*

4 tbsp melted butter
3 tsp swerve brown sugar
1 cup fresh blackberries
1 tsp vanilla extract

1 lemon, juiced
1 cup ricotta cheese
3 to 4 fresh basil leaves to garnish
1 egg, lightly beaten

## Directions:

Preheat the oven to 350 F and grease a pie pan with cooking spray

To make the piecrust: in a large bowl, mix the almond flour, coconut flour, and salt. Add the butter and mix with an electric hand mixer until crumbly. Add the erythritol and vanilla extract until mixed in. Pour in the 4 eggs one after another while mixing until formed into a ball.

Flatten the dough a clean flat surface, cover in plastic wrap, and refrigerate for 1 hour.

After, lightly dust a clean flat surface with almond flour, unwrap the dough, and roll out the dough into a 1-inch diameter circle.

*For the filling:*

In a 10-inch shallow baking pan, mix the butter, swerve brown sugar, blackberries, vanilla extract, and lemon juice. Arrange the blackberries uniformly across the pan.

Lay the pastry over the fruit filling and tuck the sides into the pan. Brush with the beaten egg and bake in the oven for 35 to 40 minutes or until the golden and puffed up.

Remove, allow cooling for 5 minutes, and then run a knife around the pan to losing the pastry. Turn the pie over onto a plate, crumble the ricotta cheese on top, and garnish with basil leaves.

## Nutritional Fact per Serving:

Calories: 465; Fat: 41.1g; Total Carbs: 7.9g; Fiber: 2.1g; Net Carbs: 5.8g; Protein: 15.9g

# Lemon Sponge Cake with Cream

Sponge cakes could be boring when served plainly. So, I made a yogurt filling topped with lemon puree to sandwich two sponge cakes to add some exciting element to the dessert and some flavor.

**PREPARATION TIME: 10 MINUTES • COOKING TIME: 30 MINUTES • SERVES: 4**

## Ingredients:

### *For the lemon puree:*

4 large lemons
¼ cup maple (sugar-free) syrup

¼ tsp salt

### *For the cake:*

½ cup unsalted butter, softened
½ cup erythritol
1 tsp vanilla extract
½ cup almond flour, sifted

3 large eggs, lightly beaten
½ cup heavy cream
1 tbsp swerve confectioner's sugar, for dusting

## Directions:

### *For the lemon puree:*

Peel and juice the lemon. Strain or remove any white strains from the peel and transfer both peels and juice to a small saucepan. Add the erythritol and salt and simmer over low heat for 30 minutes. Pour the mixture into a blender and process until smooth. Pour into a jar and set aside.

### *For the cake:*

Preheat the oven to 350 F, grease a two (2 x 8 inch) springform pans with cooking spray, and line with parchment paper.

In a large mixing bowl, cream the butter, erythritol, and vanilla extract with an electric whisk until light and fluffy. Pour in the eggs gradually while beating until fully mixed. Carefully fold in the almond flour and share the mixture into the cake pans.

Bake in the oven for 25 to 30 minutes or until springy when touched and a toothpick inserted comes out clean.

Remove and allow cooling in the pans for 5 minutes before turning out onto a wire rack.

In a bowl, whip the double cream until a soft peak forms. Spoon onto the bottom sides of the cake and spread the lemon puree on top. Sandwich both cakes and sift the confectioner's sugar on top. Slice and serve.

## Nutritional Fact per Serving:

Calories: 266; Fat: 24.9g; Total Carbs: 4.8g; Fiber: 0.2g; Net Carbs: 4.6g; Protein: 6.6g

# Cranberry Coconut Parfait

For a quick dessert option, this parfait is a go-to. Just layer these easily available ingredients and enjoy a dessert like a king.

**PREPARATION TIME: 5 MINUTES • SERVES: 4**

## Ingredients:

2 cups coconut yogurt

¼ cup fresh cranberries

½ lemon, zested

3 mint sprigs, leaves extracted and chopped

2 tbsp hemp seeds

Maple (sugar-free) syrup to taste

## Directions:

In a medium serving glasses, layer half of the coconut yogurt, cranberries, lemon zest, mint, hemp seeds, and drizzle with maple syrup. Repeat with a second layer. Serve with maple syrup.

## Nutritional Fact per Serving:

Calories: 105; Fat: 7.8g; Total Carbs: 4.5g; Fiber: 1.5g; Net Carbs: 2.9g; Protein: 5.2g

# Dark Chocolate Fudge

Easy posy with dark chocolate for 100% yumminess.

**PREPARATION TIME: 10 MINUTES • COOKING TIME: 20 MINUTES • SERVES: 4**

## Ingredients:

4 large eggs

1 cup swerve sugar

1 cup unsweetened dark chocolate, melted

½ cup melted butter

1/3 cup coconut flour

## Directions:

Preheat the oven to 350 F and line a rectangular baking tray with parchment paper.

In a large mixing bowl, cream the eggs with swerve sugar until smooth. Add the melted chocolate, butter, and whisk until evenly combined. Carefully fold in the coconut flour to incorporate and pour the mixture into the baking tray.

Bake in the oven for 20 minutes or until a toothpick inserted comes out clean.

Remove from the oven and allow cooling in the tray. After, cut into squares and serve.

## Nutritional Fact per Serving:

Calories: 491 ; Fat: 45.1g; Total Carbs: 8.5g; Fiber: 5.7g; Net Carbs: 2.8g; Protein: 11.3g

# Creamy Avocado Drink

This drink will wash down any of these meals excellently. It is rich and my best recommendation for any keto drink options that you seek to try.

**PREPARATION TIME: 5 MINUTES • SERVES: 4**

## Ingredients:

4 large ripe avocados, halved and pitted
4 tbsp swerve sugar
¼ cup cold almond milk
1 tsp vanilla extract
1 tbsp cold heavy cream

## Directions:

In a blender, add the avocado pulp, swerve sugar, almond milk, vanilla extract, and heavy cream. Process until smooth.

Pour the mixture into 2 tall serving glasses, garnish with strawberries, and serve immediately.

## Nutritional Fact per Serving:

Calories: 388; Fat: 32.1g; Total Carbs: 5.4g; Fiber: 3.3g; Net Carbs: 2.1g; Protein: 6.9g

Made in the USA
Middletown, DE
16 August 2019